JavaScript JSON Cookbook

Over 80 recipes to make the most of JSON in your desktop, server, web, and mobile applications

Ray Rischpater

BIRMINGHAM - MUMBAI

JavaScript JSON Cookbook

First published: June 2015

Production reference: 1230615

Published by Packt Publishing Ltd.
Livery Place
35 Livery Street
Birmingham B3 2PB, UK.

ISBN 978-1-78528-690-2

www.packtpub.com

Credits

Author
Ray Rischpater

Reviewers
Vipul A M

Robert MacLean

Charlotte Spencer

Commissioning Editor
Amarabha Banerjee

Acquisition Editors
Manish Nainani

Llewellyn Rozario

Content Development Editor
Susmita Sabat

Technical Editor
Ankur Ghiye

Copy Editor
Adithi Shetty

Project Coordinator
Suzanne Coutinho

Proofreader
Safis Editing

Indexer
Priya Sane

Production Coordinator
Shantanu N. Zagade

Cover Work
Shantanu N. Zagade

About the Author

Ray Rischpater is an engineer and author with over 20 years of experience in writing about and developing for mobile computing platforms.

During this time, he participated in the development of Internet technologies and custom applications for Java ME, Qualcomm BREW, Apple iPhone, Google Android, Palm OS, Newton, and Magic Cap, as well as several proprietary platforms. Currently, he's employed as a software development manager at Microsoft in Sunnyvale, where he works on mapping and data visualization.

When he is not writing about software development, he enjoys hiking and photography with his family and friends in and around the San Lorenzo Valley in Central California. When he can, he also provides public service through amateur radio as the licensed Amateur Extra station KF6GPE.

Among the books he's written are *Application Development with Qt Creator* (now in its second edition, published by *Packt Publishing*, 2014) and *Microsoft Mapping* (with *Carmen Au*, published by *Apress*, 2013). Ray also irregularly blog at `http://www.lothlorien.com/kf6gpe`.

Ray holds a bachelor's degree in pure mathematics from the University of California, Santa Cruz, and is a member of the IEEE, ACM, and ARRL.

About the Reviewers

Vipul A M works as a software developer at BigBinary LLC. He is an avid Rails on Ruby projects contributor. He spends his spare time exploring and contributing to many open source Ruby projects when not dabbling with ReactJS or creating various screencasts.

He is currently working on a book titled *ReactJS by Example*, which walks you through how to use ReactJS, while working on project examples.

Vipul loves Ruby's vibrant community and helps in building PuneRb. He is the founder of and runs the RubyIndia Community newsletter and RubyIndia podcast and organizes the Deccan Ruby Conference in Pune. He blogs prolifically at `blog.bigbinary.com` and loves doing various screencasts at `videos.bigbinary.com`.

Robert MacLean has been working for over 18 years as a developer and an IT professional in South Africa, where he worked on a wide variety of projects with a number of customers. Today, he works as a developer at Microsoft, developing applications for Windows platforms.

Charlotte Spencer is a frontend web developer with a keen interest in semantic HTML, progressive enhancement, and accessibility. When they're not programming, they are writing about the Web and her experiences with it, reading, or preparing for the zombie apocalypse. They tweets at `@charlotteis`.

www.PacktPub.com

Support files, eBooks, discount offers, and more

For support files and downloads related to your book, please visit www.PacktPub.com.

Did you know that Packt offers eBook versions of every book published, with PDF and ePub files available? You can upgrade to the eBook version at www.PacktPub.com and as a print book customer, you are entitled to a discount on the eBook copy. Get in touch with us at service@packtpub.com for more details.

At www.PacktPub.com, you can also read a collection of free technical articles, sign up for a range of free newsletters and receive exclusive discounts and offers on Packt books and eBooks.

https://www2.packtpub.com/books/subscription/packtlib

Do you need instant solutions to your IT questions? PacktLib is Packt's online digital book library. Here, you can search, access, and read Packt's entire library of books.

Why Subscribe?

- ▶ Fully searchable across every book published by Packt
- ▶ Copy and paste, print, and bookmark content
- ▶ On demand and accessible via a web browser

Free Access for Packt account holders

If you have an account with Packt at www.PacktPub.com, you can use this to access PacktLib today and view 9 entirely free books. Simply use your login credentials for immediate access.

Table of Contents

Preface

JavaScript Object Notation (JSON) has rapidly become the lingua franca for structured document exchange on the Web, outpacing XML in many domains. Three of the reasons for this are obvious: it plays well with JavaScript, it's simple, and it just works. However, there are other reasons for its success as well. As you'll see in the pages of this book, it's supported by a wide variety of languages and libraries, making it easy to use in all kinds of scenarios.

In this book, I provide recipes for common uses of JSON. You're welcome to read the book from cover to cover, seeing all the ways JSON can be used in building web and standalone applications. However, it's organized as a cookbook, so that you can quickly go to the chapter or recipe that addresses a particular problem you might want to solve with JSON now. I recommend skimming this preface to see what's where, taking a quick look at *Chapter 1, Reading and Writing JSON on the Client*, or *Chapter 2, Reading and Writing JSON on the Server*, depending on your interest, and then jumping right to the recipes that interest you the most.

What this book covers

Chapter 1, Reading and Writing JSON on the Client, gives you recipes to read and write JSON in a number of client environments, including JavaScript, C#, C++, Java, Perl, and Python.

Chapter 2, Reading and Writing JSON on the Server, goes the other way, looking at JSON on typical server-side languages such as Clojure, C#, Node.js, PHP, and Ruby. Of course, you can write client-side applications with these languages, as well, just as you can write a server in C# or Java. So the division of recipes between these chapters is somewhat arbitrary; pick a language and dive in!

Chapter 3, Using JSON in Simple AJAX Applications, shows you how to apply JSON for data exchange with today's browsers.

Chapter 4, Using JSON in AJAX Applications with jQuery and AngularJS, discusses how to use JSON with two popular web frameworks, jQuery and Angular.

Chapter 5, Using JSON with MongoDB, shows you how MongoDB, a popular NoSQL database, uses JSON for its stored document format and gives you recipes to use MongoDB as a REST service in your web applications.

Chapter 6, Using JSON with CouchDB, shows you how CouchDB, another popular NoSQL database, uses JSON and how you can use CouchDB as a standalone REST service in your web applications.

Chapter 7, Using JSON in a Type-safe Manner, looks at how you can adapt the type-free nature of JSON with the type safety provided by languages such as C#, Java, and TypeScript to reduce programming errors in your application.

Chapter 8, Using JSON for Binary Data Transfer, shows you how, even though JSON is a text-based document format, you can still use it to move binary data around if you have to do so.

Chapter 9, Querying JSON with JSONPath and LINQ, has recipes on how you can write queries against JSON documents to obtain just the slice of data you're looking for. This is especially powerful when combined with the recipes from *Chapters 5, Using JSON with MongoDB*, and *Chapter 6, Using JSON with CouchDB*.

Chapter 10, JSON on Mobile Platforms, shows you recipes for using JSON in mobile applications that use Android, iOS, and Qt.

What you need for this book

Unlike many other technical books, this one focuses on a wide variety of supporting technologies in its examples. I don't expect that you'll have experience or the tools to try every example in this book, especially right away. However, it's helpful to have a few things set out.

You should have some programming experience, preferably in JavaScript. Unless a recipe is targeted at a specific programming language such as C#, the recipes in this book are written in JavaScript. I do this for two reasons. Firstly because the "J" in JSON stands for JavaScript (even though it's widely applicable to other languages), and, in this day and age, every programmer should have at least a nodding familiarity of JavaScript.

As far as software environments go, to begin with, you should have access to a good web browser such as Chrome or a recent version of Safari, Firefox, or Internet Explorer. You can use the JavaScript runtime in any of these browsers to experiment with JSON and get started.

Secondly, a lot of the client-server examples feature Node.js. I picked Node.js for server-side example programming because it's also JavaScript, meaning that you don't have to jump through different language syntaxes as you move between the client and server. Node.js runs well on Windows, Mac OS X, and Linux, too, so you shouldn't have a problem setting it up.

If you're interested in using JSON with databases, CouchDB or MongoDB are your best choices and I discuss both of them in this book. Which one you choose is really a matter of your domain and personal preference. I've been using MongoDB for 5 years on various projects but have recently taken a liking to some of CouchDB's features and its integrated support for RESTful services.

Finally, if you're a Microsoft developer, you may want to take special note of the C# examples that use Newtonsoft's Json.NET throughout this book. Json.NET is what JSON in C# ought to be, and it's definitely worth your attention.

Who this book is for

If you're writing applications that move structured data from one place to another, this book is for you. This is especially true if you've been using XML to do the job because it's entirely possible that you could do much of the same work with less code and less data overhead in JSON.

While the book's chapters make some distinction between the client and server sides of an application, it doesn't matter if you're a frontend, backend, or full-stack developer. The principles behind using JSON apply to both the client and the server, and in fact, developers who understand both sides of the equation generally craft the best applications.

Sections

In this book, you will find several headings that appear frequently (Getting ready, How to do it, How it works, There's more, and See also).

To give clear instructions on how to complete a recipe, we use these sections as follows:

Getting ready

This section tells you what to expect in the recipe, and describes how to set up any software or any preliminary settings required for the recipe.

How to do it...

This section contains the steps required to follow the recipe.

How it works...

This section usually consists of a detailed explanation of what happened in the previous section.

There's more...

This section consists of additional information about the recipe in order to make the reader more knowledgeable about the recipe.

See also

This section provides helpful links to other useful information for the recipe.

Conventions

In this book, you will find a number of text styles that distinguish between different kinds of information. Here are some examples of these styles and an explanation of their meaning.

Code words in text, database table names, folder names, filenames, file extensions, pathnames, dummy URLs, user input, and Twitter handles are shown as follows: "Let's look at `loads` and `dumps` further."

A block of code is set as follows:

```
function doAjax() {
var xmlhttp;
  if (window.XMLHttpRequest)
  {
    // code for IE7+, Firefox, Chrome, Opera, Safari
    xmlhttp=new XMLHttpRequest();
  }
}
```

When we wish to draw your attention to a particular part of a code block, the relevant lines or items are set in bold:

```
function doAjax() {
var xmlhttp;
  if (window.XMLHttpRequest)
  {
    // code for IE7+, Firefox, Chrome, Opera, Safari
    xmlhttp=new XMLHttpRequest();
  }
}
```

Any command-line input or output is written as follows:

```
# cp /usr/src/asterisk-addons/configs/cdr_mysql.conf.sample
    /etc/asterisk/cdr_mysql.conf
```

New terms and **important words** are shown in bold. Words that you see on the screen, for example, in menus or dialog boxes, appear in the text like this: " Then, you'll want to go to **More Tools | JavaScript console**."

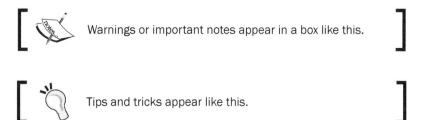

Warnings or important notes appear in a box like this.

Tips and tricks appear like this.

Reader feedback

Feedback from our readers is always welcome. Let us know what you think about this book—what you liked or disliked. Reader feedback is important for us as it helps us develop titles that you will really get the most out of.

To send us general feedback, simply e-mail feedback@packtpub.com, and mention the book's title in the subject of your message.

If there is a topic that you have expertise in and you are interested in either writing or contributing to a book, see our author guide at www.packtpub.com/authors.

Customer support

Now that you are the proud owner of a Packt book, we have a number of things to help you to get the most from your purchase.

Downloading the example code

You can download the example code files from your account at http://www.packtpub.com for all the Packt Publishing books you have purchased. If you purchased this book elsewhere, you can visit http://www.packtpub.com/support and register to have the files e-mailed directly to you.

Errata

Although we have taken every care to ensure the accuracy of our content, mistakes do happen. If you find a mistake in one of our books—maybe a mistake in the text or the code—we would be grateful if you could report this to us. By doing so, you can save other readers from frustration and help us improve subsequent versions of this book. If you find any errata, please report them by visiting `http://www.packtpub.com/submit-errata`, selecting your book, clicking on the **Errata Submission Form** link, and entering the details of your errata. Once your errata are verified, your submission will be accepted and the errata will be uploaded to our website or added to any list of existing errata under the Errata section of that title.

To view the previously submitted errata, go to `https://www.packtpub.com/books/content/support` and enter the name of the book in the search field. The required information will appear under the **Errata** section.

Piracy

Piracy of copyrighted material on the Internet is an ongoing problem across all media. At Packt, we take the protection of our copyright and licenses very seriously. If you come across any illegal copies of our works in any form on the Internet, please provide us with the location address or website name immediately so that we can pursue a remedy.

Please contact us at `copyright@packtpub.com` with a link to the suspected pirated material.

We appreciate your help in protecting our authors and our ability to bring you valuable content.

Questions

If you have a problem with any aspect of this book, you can contact us at `questions@packtpub.com`, and we will do our best to address the problem.

1
Reading and Writing JSON on the Client

In this chapter, we will cover the following recipes:

- ▶ Reading and writing JSON in JavaScript
- ▶ Reading and writing JSON in C++
- ▶ Reading and writing JSON in C#
- ▶ Reading and writing JSON in Java
- ▶ Reading and writing JSON in Perl
- ▶ Reading and writing JSON in Python

In addition to reading and writing JSON in Python, we will begin by showing you a brief review of JSON formatting to help set the stage for what follows in this book.

Introduction

JSON stands for **JavaScript Object Notation**. It's an open standard to represent data as attributes with values. Originally derived from the JavaScript syntax (hence its name) for use in web applications as an alternative to the more verbose and structured **Extensible Markup Language** (**XML**), it is now used for data serialization and transport in many standalone and web applications.

JSON provides an ideal means to encapsulate data between the client and server. In this first chapter, you will learn how to work with JSON in languages specified at the beginning of this chapter.

These languages are often used for client-side development, which is what we will focus on here. We'll look more at server-side languages in *Chapter 2, Reading and Writing JSON on the Server*.

Let's take a look at some JSON returned by the web API, available at `http://www.aprs.fi`, and modified a bit by me to make the example clear (later, in *Chapter 4, Using JSON in AJAX Applications with jQuery and AngularJS*, you'll learn how to fetch this data yourself using a web browser and JavaScript):

```json
{
    "command":"get",
    "result":"ok",
    "what":"loc",
    "found":2,
    "entries":[
      {
        "class":"a",
        "name":"KF6GPE",
        "type":"l",
        "time":"1399371514",
        "lasttime":"1418597513",
        "lat":37.17667,
        "lng":-122.14650,
        "symbol":"\/-",
        "srccall":"KF6GPE",
      },
      {
        "class":"a",
        "name":"KF6GPE-7",
        "type":"l",
        "time":"1418591475",
        "lasttime":"1418591475",
        "lat":37.17633,
        "lng":-122.14583,
        "symbol":"\\K",
        "srccall":"KF6GPE-7",
      }
    ]
}
```

Downloading the example code

You can download the example code files from your account at `http://www.packtpub.com` for all the Packt Publishing books you have purchased. If you purchased this book elsewhere, you can visit `http://www.packtpub.com/support` and register to have the files e-mailed directly to you.

There are a few things to notice about this example:

- ▸ The data is organized into attributes and values, each separated by a colon. (Note that a JSON document can also be a single value, such as a string, float, integer, or Boolean value.)

- ▸ Attributes appear as character strings enclosed by double quotes on the left-hand side of a colon.

- ▸ Values are on the right side of the colon and can be the following:

  - ❏ Character strings (enclosed in double quotes) such as `KF6GPE`

  - ❏ Numbers (either integers or floating point) such as `2` or `37.17667`

  - ❏ Arrays (comma-delimited values contained in square brackets), such as the value for `entries`

  - ❏ Whole objects consisting of more attributes and values, such as the two-array values in the `entries` value

  - ❏ Alternatively (although this example doesn't show it), the Boolean values `true` and `false`

- ▸ Note that many other kinds of values, such as date/time pairs or individual characters are not supported by JSON.

- ▸ Although it's not entirely clear from this example, whitespace is insignificant. There's no need to have each pair on its own line, for example, and the indentation is completely arbitrary.

The attribute-name-attribute-value property of JSON, along with the ability to nest values and represent arrays, gives JSON a lot of flexibility. You can represent a lot of common objects using JSON, including most objects that don't have a lot of binary data (For ideas on how to represent binary data using JavaScript and JSON, see *Chapter 8, Using JSON for Binary Data Transfer*). This includes primitive values (self-documenting because each value is accompanied by an attribute), flat objects with simple values including maps, and arrays of simple or complex objects.

The self-documenting nature of JSON makes it an ideal choice for data transport as you develop new objects, despite its lack of support for comments as you might find in XML. Its plaintext nature makes it amenable to compression over the wire using popular compression schemes such as `gzip` (available inside most web servers and web clients), and its format is easier for humans to read than the more verbose XML.

Note that JSON documents are inherently trees, and thus, do not have support for cyclical data structures, such as graphs, where a node points to another node in the same data structure.

If you create such a data structure using the native representation in the programming language you're using and try to convert that to JSON, you'll get an error.

Reading and writing JSON in JavaScript

JSON originated as a means to carry data between web servers and JavaScript, so let's begin with a simple code snippet that reads and writes JSON in JavaScript in a web browser. We'll show the entirety of a web application using AJAX and JSON in *Chapter 4, Using JSON in AJAX Applications with jQuery and AngularJS*; what follows is how to obtain a JavaScript object from JSON and how to create a JSON string from a JavaScript object.

Getting ready

You'll need a way to edit the JavaScript and run it in your browser. In this example, and nearly all examples in this book, we'll use Google Chrome for this. You can download Google Chrome at `https://www.google.com/chrome/browser`. Once you install Google Chrome, you'll want to activate the JavaScript console by clicking on the **Customize and control Doodle Chrome** icon on the right-hand side, which looks like this:

Then, you'll want to go to **More Tools | JavaScript console**. You should see a JavaScript console on the side of the web page, like this:

If you prefer key commands, you can also use *Ctrl* + *Shift* + *J* on Windows and Linux, or *control* + *option* + *J* on a Macintosh.

From here, you can enter JavaScript on the lower right-hand corner and press *Enter* (*return* on a Mac OS X system) to evaluate the JavaScript.

How to do it...

Modern web browsers, such as Chrome, define a JSON object in the JavaScript runtime that can convert the string data containing JSON to JavaScript objects, and convert a JavaScript object to JSON. Here's a simple example:

```
>var json = '{"call":"KF6GPE","type":"1","time":
"1399371514","lasttime":"1418597513","lat":37.17667,"lng":
-122.14650,"result" : "ok" }';
<- "{ "call":"KF6GPE","type":"1","time":"1399371514",
"lasttime":"1418597513","lat":37.17667,"lng":-122.14650,
"result" : "ok" }"
>var object = JSON.parse(json);
<- Object {call:"KF6GPE",type:"1",time:"1399371514",
lasttime:"1418597513",lat:37.17667, lng:-122.14650,result: "ok"}
> object.result
<- "ok"
>var newJson = JSON.stringify(object);
<- "{ "call":"KF6GPE","type":"1","time":"1399371514",
"lasttime":"1418597513","lat": 37.17667,"lng": -122.14650,
"result" : "ok" }"
```

 In this and subsequent JavaScript examples, the text you type in the JavaScript console is preceded by a > symbol, while what the JavaScript console prints is anything beginning with <- symbol.

How it works...

Chrome and other modern web browsers define the JSON object, which has methods to convert between strings containing JSON and JavaScript objects.

In the previous example, we begin by setting the value of the json variable to a simple JSON expression consisting of one attribute result with the value ok. The JavaScript interpreter returns the resulting value of the variable json.

The next line uses the JSON method parse to convert the JSON string referenced by json into a JavaScript object:

```
>var object = JSON.parse(json);
<- Object { call:"KF6GPE", type:"1", time:"1399371514",
lasttime:"1418597513", lat:37.17667, lng:-122.14650, result: "ok"}
```

You can then access any of the values in the object, just as you would any other JavaScript object; it is, after all, just an object:

```
> object.result;
<- "ok"
```

Finally, if you need to convert an object to JSON, you can do that with the JSON method stringify:

```
>var newJson = JSON.stringify(object);
<- "{ "call":"KF6GPE","type":"1","time":"1399371514",
"lasttime":"1418597513","lat": 37.17667,"lng": -122.14650,
"result" : "ok" }"
```

There's more...

You should know two things about these methods. First of all, parse will throw an exception if the JSON you pass is malformed, or isn't JSON at all:

```
>JSON.parse('{"result" = "ok" }')
<- VM465:2 Uncaught SyntaxError: Unexpected token =
```

The errors aren't very helpful but better than nothing if you're debugging JSON sent by a less-than-fully compliant and debugged JSON encoder.

Second, very old web browsers may not have a JSON object with these methods. In that case, you can use the JavaScript function eval after wrapping the JSON in parenthesis, like this:

```
>eval('('+json+')')
<- Object {result: "ok"}
```

The eval function evaluates the string you pass as JavaScript, and the JSON notation is really just a subset of JavaScript. However, you should avoid using eval whenever you can for a few reasons. First, it's often slower than the methods provided by the JSON object. Second, it's not safe; your string might contain malicious JavaScript that can crash or otherwise subvert your JavaScript application, which is not a threat you should take lightly. Use the JSON object whenever it's available. Third, you can use the parse and stringify methods to handle simple values, such as Booleans, numbers, and strings; you're not limited to the key-value pairs in the previous example. If all I wanted to do was pass a Boolean (such as "the transaction succeeded!"), I might just write the following:

```
var jsonSuccess = 'true';
<- "true"
> var flag = JSON.parse(jsonSuccess);
```

Finally, it's worth pointing out that both the `parse` and `stringify` methods to JSON take an optional replacer function, which is invoked on every key and value in the object being serialized or deserialized. You can use this function to perform on-the-fly data conversions as the JSON is being parsed; for example, you can use it to convert between the string representation of a date and the number of seconds since midnight at the start of the epoch, or to correct the capitalization of strings. I could use a replacer function for either side of the transformation, as shown in the following code, to make the call field lowercase:

```
> var object = JSON.parse(json, function(k, v) {
   if ( k == 'call') return v.toLowerCase();
});
<- Object { call:"kf6gpe", type:"l", time:"1399371514",
lasttime:"1418597513", lat:37.17667, lng:-122.14650, result: "ok"}
```

You can also return `undefined` to remove an item from the results; to omit the type field from the JSON I generate, I can execute the following:

```
> var newJson = JSON.stringify(object, function (k, v) {
   if k == 'type') return undefined;
});
<- "{ "call":"KF6GPE","time":"1399371514","lasttime":
"1418597513","lat": 37.17667,"lng": -122.14650, "result" : "ok"
}"
```

Reading and writing JSON in C++

C++ is a language that long-predates JSON, but is still relevant for many projects. There's no native support for JSON in C++ but there are a number of libraries that provide support for working with JSON. Perhaps the most widely used is **JsonCpp**, available from GitHub at `https://github.com/open-source-parsers/jsoncpp`. It's licensed under the MIT license or public domain if you so desire, so there are virtually no limitations on its use.

Getting ready

To use JsonCpp, you need to first go to the website and download the zip file with the entire library. Once you do so, you need to integrate it with your application's source code.

How you integrate it with your application's source code differs from platform to platform, but the general process is this:

1. Create an amalgamated source and header for the library using the instructions on the website. To do this, you'll need to have JsonCpp downloaded and Python 2.6 or later installed. From the top level directory of JsonCpp, run `python amalgamate.py`.

2. Include the include file `dist/json/json.h` in any file where you want to use the JsonCpp library.

3. Include the source file `dist/jsoncpp.cpp` in your project's make file or build system.

Once you do this, you should have access to the JsonCpp interface in any file that includes the `json/json.h` header.

How to do it...

Here's a simple C++ application that uses JsonCpp to convert between `std::string` containing some simple JSON and a JSON object:

```cpp
#include <string>
#include <iostream>
#include "json/json.h"

using namespace std;

int main(int argc, _TCHAR* argv[])
{
  Json::Reader reader;
  Json::Value root;

  string json = "{\"call\": \"KF6GPE\",\"type\":\"1\",\"time\":
  \"1399371514\",\"lasttime\":\"1418597513\",\"lat\": 37.17667,
  \"lng\": -122.14650,\"result\":\"ok\"}";

  bool parseSuccess = reader.parse(json, root, false);

  if (parseSuccess)
  {
    const Json::Value resultValue = root["result"];
    cout << "Result is " << resultValue.asString() << "\n";
  }

  Json::StyledWriter styledWriter;
  Json::FastWriter fastWriter;
  Json::Value newValue;
  newValue["result"] = "ok";

  cout << styledWriter.write(newValue) << "\n";
  cout << fastWriter.write(newValue) << "\n";

  return 0;
}
```

How it works...

This example begins by including the necessary includes, including `json/json.h`, which defines the interface to JsonCpp. We explicitly reference the `std` namespace for brevity, although don't do so for the `Json` namespace, in which JsonCpp defines all of its interfaces.

The JsonCpp implementation defines `Json::Reader` and `Json::Writer`, specifying the interfaces to JSON readers and writers, respectively. In practice, the `Json::Reader` interface is also the implementation of a JSON class that can read JSON, returning its values as `Json::Value`. The `Json::Writer` variable just defines an interface; you'll want to use a subclass of it such as `Json::FastWriter` or `Json::StyledWriter` to create JSON from `Json::Value` objects.

The previous listing begins by defining `Json::Reader` and `Json::Value`; we'll use the reader to read the JSON we define on the next line and store its value in the `Json::Value` variable `root`. (Presumably your C++ application would get its JSON from another source, such as a web service or local file.)

Parsing JSON is as simple as calling the reader's `parse` function, passing the JSON and `Json::Value` into which it will write the JSON values. It returns a Boolean, which will be `true` if the JSON parsing succeeds.

The `Json::Value` class represents the JSON object as a tree; individual values are referenced by the attribute name in the original JSON, and the values are the values of those keys, accessible through methods such as `asString`, which returns the value of the object as a native C++ type. These methods of `Json::Value` includes the following:

- `asString`, which returns `std::string`
- `asInt`, which returns `Int`
- `asUInt`, which returns `UInt`
- `asInt64`, which returns `Int64`
- `asFloat`, which returns `float`
- `asDouble`, which returns `double`
- `asBool`, which returns `bool`

In addition, the class provides `operator[]`, letting you access array elements.

You can also query a `Json::Value` object to determine its type using one of these methods:

- `isNull`, which returns `true` if the value is `null`
- `isBool`, which returns `true` if the value is `bool`
- `isInt`, which returns `true` if the value is `Int`
- `isUInt`, which returns `true` if the value is `UInt`

- ▶ `isIntegral`, which returns `true` if the value is an integer
- ▶ `isDouble`, which returns `true` if the value is `double`
- ▶ `isNumeric`, which returns `true` if the value is numeric
- ▶ `isString`, which returns `true` if the value is a string
- ▶ `isArray`, which returns `true` if the value is an array
- ▶ `isObject`, which returns true if the value is another JSON object (which you can decompose using another `Json::Value` value)

At any rate, our code uses `asString` to fetch the `std::string` value encoded as the `result` attribute, and writes it to the console.

The code then defines `Json::StyledWriter` and `Json::FastWriter` to create some pretty-printed JSON and unformatted JSON in strings, as well as a single `Json::Value` object to contain our new JSON. Assigning content to the JSON value is simple because it overrides the `operator[]` and `operator[]=` methods with the appropriate implementations to convert standard C++ types to JSON objects. So, the following line of code creates a single JSON attribute/value pair with the attribute set to `result`, and the value set to `ok` (although this code doesn't show it, you can create trees of JSON attribute-value pairs by assigning JSON objects to other JSON objects):

```
newValue["result"] = "ok";
```

We first use `StyledWriter` and then `FastWriter` to encode the JSON value in `newValue`, writing each string to the console.

Of course, you can also pass single values to JsonCpp; there's no reason why you can't execute the following code if all you wanted to do was pass a double-precision number:

```
Json::Reader reader;
Json::Value piValue;

string json = "3.1415";
bool parseSuccess = reader.parse(json, piValue, false);
   double pi = piValue.asDouble();
```

See also

For the documentation for JsonCpp, you can install doxygen from `http://www.stack.nl/~dimitri/doxygen/` and run it over the `doc` folder of the main JsonCpp distribution.

There are other JSON conversion implementations for C++, too. For a complete list, see the list at `http://json.org/`.

Reading and writing JSON in C#

C# is a common client-side language for rich applications as well as for writing the client implementation of web services running on ASP.NET. The .NET library includes JSON serialization and deserialization in the System.Web.Extensions assembly.

Getting ready

This example uses the built-in JSON serializer and deserializer in the System.Web.Extensions assembly, one of the many .NET libraries that are available. If you've installed a recent version of Visual Studio (see `https://www.visualstudio.com/en-us/downloads/visual-studio-2015-downloads-vs.aspx`), it should be available. All you need to do to use this assembly is include it in the assemblies your application references in Visual Studio by right-clicking the **References** item in your project, choosing **Add Reference**, and scrolling down to **System.Web.Extensions** in the **Framework Assemblies** list.

How to do it...

Here's a simple application that deserializes some JSON, as a dictionary of attribute-object pairs:

```
using System;
using System.Collections.Generic;
using System.Web.Script.Serialization;

namespace JSONExample
{
    public class SimpleResult
    {
        public string result;
    }

    class Program
    {
        static void Main(string[] args)
        {
            JavaScriptSerializer serializer =
            new System.Web.Script.Serialization.
            JavaScriptSerializer();

            string json = @"{ ""call"":""KF6GPE"",""type"":
""l"",""time"":""1399371514"",""lasttime"":""1418597513"",
""lat"": 37.17667,""lng\"": -122.14650,""result"": ""ok"" }";
```

```
dynamic result = serializer.DeserializeObject(json);
        foreach (KeyValuePair<string, object> entry in result)
        {
            var key = entry.Key;
            var value = entry.Value as string;
Console.WriteLine(String.Format("{0} : {1}",
key, value));
        }
        Console.WriteLine(serializer.Serialize(result));

        var anotherResult = new SimpleResult { result="ok" };
        Console.WriteLine(serializer.Serialize(
        anotherResult));
    }
  }
}
```

How it works...

The System.Web.Extensions assembly provides the `JavaScriptSerializer` class in the `System.Web.Script.Serialization` namespace. This code begins by defining a simple class, `SimpleResult`, which we'll encode as JSON in our example.

The `Main` method first defines a `JavaScriptSerializer` instance, and then `string` containing our JSON. Parsing the JSON is as easy as calling the `JavaScriptSerializer` instance's `DeserializeObject` method, which returns an object whose type is determined at run-time based on the JSON you pass.

> You can also use `DeserializeObject` to parse JSON in a type-safe manner, and then the type of the returned object matches the type you pass to the method. I'll show you how to do this in *Chapter 7, Using JSON in a Type-safe Manner*.

`DeserializeObject` returns a `Dictionary` of key-value pairs; the keys are the attributes in the JSON, and the values are objects representing the values of those attributes. In our example, we simply walk the keys and values in the dictionary, printing each. Because we know the type of the value in the JSON, we can simply cast it to the appropriate type (`string`, in this case) using the C# as keyword; if it wasn't `string`, we'd receive the value `null`. You can use `as` or the type inference of C# to determine the type of unknown objects in your JSON, making it easy to parse JSON for which you lack strict semantics.

The `JavaScriptSerializer` class also includes a `Serialize` method; you can either pass it as a dictionary of attribute-value pairs, as we do with our deserialized result, or you can pass it as an instance of a C# class. If you pass it as a class, it'll attempt to serialize the class by introspecting the class fields and values.

There's more...

The JSON implementation that Microsoft provides is adequate for many purposes, but not necessarily the best for your application. Other developers have implemented better ones that typically use the same interface as the Microsoft implementation. One good choice is Newtonsoft's Json.NET, which you can get at `http://json.codeplex.com/` or from NuGet in Visual Studio. It supports a wider variety of .NET platforms (including Windows Phone), LINQ queries, XPath-like queries against the JSON, and is faster than the Microsoft implementation. Using it is similar to using the Microsoft implementation: install the package from the Web or NuGet, add a reference of the assembly to your application, and then use the `JsonSerializer` class in the `NewtonSoft.Json` namespace. It defines the same `SerializeObject` and `DeserializeObject` methods that the Microsoft implementation does, making switching to this library easy. *James Newton-King*, the author of *Json.NET*, makes it available under the MIT license.

As with other languages, you can also carry primitive types through the deserialization and serialization process. For example, after evaluating the following code, the resulting dynamic variable `piResult` will contain a floating-point number, 3.14:

```
string piJson = "3.14";
dynamic piResult = serializer.DeserializeObject(piJson);
```

See also

As I previously hinted, you can do this in a type-safe manner; we'll discuss more of this in *Chapter 7, Using JSON in a Type-safe Manner*. You'll do this using the generic method `DeserializeObject<>`, passing a type variable of the type you want to deserialize into.

Reading and writing JSON in Java

Java, like C++, predates JSON. Oracle is presently working on adding JSON support to Java, but in the meantime, several implementations providing JSON support are available on the Web. Similar to the C++ implementation you saw previously in this chapter, you can convert between JSON and Java using a third-party library; in this case, packaged as a Java archive (JAR) file, whose implementation typically represents JSON objects as a tree of named objects.

Perhaps the best Java implementation of JSON parsing is Gson, available from Google at `http://code.google.com/p/google-gson/` licensed under the Apache License 2.0.

Getting ready

First, you'll need to get Gson; you can do this by doing a read-only checkout of the repository using SVN over HTTP with SVN by using the following command:

```
svn checkout http://google-gson.googlecode.com/svn/trunk/google-gson
-read-only
```

Of course, this assumes that you have a Java development kit (`http://www.oracle.com/technetwork/java/javase/downloads/index.html`) and SVN (TortoiseSVN is a good client for Windows available at `http://tortoisesvn.net/downloads.html`) installed. Many Java IDEs include support for SVN.

Once you check out the code, follow the instructions that come with it to build the Gson JAR file, and add the JAR file to your project.

How to do it...

To begin, you need to create a `com.google.gson.Gson` object. This class defines the interface you'll use to convert between JSON and Java:

```
Gson gson = new com.google.gson.Gson();
String json = "{\"call\": \"KF6GPE\", \"type\": \"1\", \"time\":
\"1399371514\", \"lasttime\": \"1418597513\", \"lat\": 37.17667,
\"lng\": -122.14650,\"result\":\"ok\"}";
com.google.gson.JsonObject result = gson.fromJson(json,
JsonElement.class).getAsJsonObject();
```

The `JsonObject` class defines the top-level object for containing a JSON object; you use its `get` and `add` methods to get and set attributes, like this:

```
JsonElement result = result.get("result").getAsString();
```

The Gson library uses the `JsonElement` class to encapsulate a single JSON value; it has the following methods that let you get the value contained in `JsonElement` as a plain Java type:

- ▶ `getAsBoolean`, which returns the value as `Boolean`
- ▶ `getAsByte`, which returns the value as `byte`
- ▶ `getAsCharacter`, which returns the value as `char`
- ▶ `getAsDouble`, which returns the value as `double`
- ▶ `getAsFloat`, which returns the value as `float`
- ▶ `getAsInt`, which returns the value as `int`
- ▶ `getAsJsonArray`, which returns the value as `JsonArray`
- ▶ `getAsJsonObject`, which returns the value as `JsonObject`

- ▸ getAsLong, which returns the value as long

- ▸ getAsShort, which returns the value as short

- ▸ getAsString, which returns the value as String

You can also learn about the type in JsonElement using one of the following methods:

- ▸ isJsonArray, which returns true if the element is an array of objects

- ▸ isJsonNull, which returns true if the element is null

- ▸ isJsonObject, which returns true if the element is a composite object (another JSON tree) instead of a single type

- ▸ isJsonPrimitive, which returns true if the element is a primitive type, such as a number or string

There's more...

You can also convert instances of your classes directly to JSON, writing something like this:

```
public class SimpleResult {
    public String result;
}

// Elsewhere in your code…
Gson gson = new com.google.gson.Gson();
SimpleResult result = new SimpleResult;
result.result = "ok";
String json = gson.toJson(result);
```

This defines a class SimpleResult, which we use to create a single instance, and then use the Gson object instance to convert to a string containing the JSON using the Gson method toJson.

Finally, because JsonElement encapsulates a single value, you can also handle simple values expressed in JSON, like this:

```
Gson gson = new com.google.gson.Gson();
String piJson = "3.14";
double result = gson.fromJson(piJson,
JsonElement.class).getAsDouble();
```

This converts the primitive value 3.14 in JSON to a Java double.

See also

Like the C# example, you can convert directly from JSON to a plain old Java object (POJO) in a type-safe manner. You'll see how to do this in *Chapter 7, Using JSON in a Type-safe Manner*.

There are other JSON conversion implementations for Java, too. For a complete list, see the list at `http://json.org/`.

Reading and writing JSON in Perl

Perl predates JSON, although there's a good implementation of JSON conversion available from CPAN, the Comprehensive Perl Archive Network.

How to do it...

To begin with, download the JSON module from CPAN and install it. Typically, you'll download the file, unpack it, and then run the following code on a system that already has Perl and make configured:

```
perl Makefile.PL
make
make install
```

Here's a simple example:

```
use JSON;
use Data::Dumper;
my $json = '{ "call":"KF6GPE","type":"l","time":"1399371514",
"lasttime":"1418597513","lat": 37.17667,"lng": -122.14650,
"result" : "ok" }';
my %result = decode_json($json);
print Dumper(result);
print encode_json(%result);
```

Let's look at the interface the JSON module provides.

How it works...

The CPAN module defines the `decode_json` and `encode_json` methods to decode and encode JSON respectively. These methods interconvert between Perl objects, such as literal values and associative arrays, and strings containing JSON respectively.

The code begins by importing the JSON and `Data::Dumper` modules. Next, it defines a single string, `$json`, which contains the JSON we want to parse.

With the JSON in `$json`, we define `%result` to be the associative array containing the objects defined in the JSON, and dump the values in the hash on the next line.

Finally, we re-encode the hash as JSON and print the results to the terminal.

See also

For more information and to download the JSON CPAN module, visit `https://metacpan.org/pod/JSON`.

Reading and writing JSON in Python

Python has had native support for JSON since Python 2.6 through the `json` module. Using the module is as simple as using the `import` statement to import the module and then accessing the encoder and decoder through the `json` object that it defines.

Getting ready

Simply enter the following in your source code to be able to reference the JSON facility:

```
import json
```

How to do it...

Here's a simple example from the Python interpreter:

```
>>> import json
>>>json = '{ "call":"KF6GPE","type":"l","time":"1399371514",
"lasttime":"1418597513","lat": 37.17667,"lng": -122.14650,
"result" : "ok" }'
u'{"call":"KF6GPE","type":"l","time":"1399371514",
"lasttime":"1418597513","lat": 37.17667,"lng": -122.14650,
"result": "ok" }'
>>>result = json.loads(json)
{u'call':u'KF6GPE',u'type':u'l',u'time':u'1399371514',
u'lasttime':u'1418597513',u'lat': 37.17667,u'lng':
-122.14650,u'result': u'ok'}
>>> result['result']
u'ok'
>>> print json.dumps(result)
{"call":"KF6GPE","type":"l","time":"1399371514",
"lasttime":"1418597513","lat": 37.17667,"lng": -122.14650,
"result":"ok"}
>>> print json.dumps(result,
```

```
...                      indent=4)
{
"call":"KF6GPE",
"type":"l",
"time":"1399371514",
"lasttime":"1418597513",
"lat": 37.17667,
"lng": -122.14650,
    "result": "ok"
}
```

Let's look at `loads` and `dumps` further.

How it works...

Python has great support for associative arrays through its object hierarchy. The `json` module offers a `json` object with `loads` and `dumps` method that convert from JSON in text strings to associative arrays, and from associative arrays to JSON in text strings. If you're familiar with the Python `marshal` and `pickle` modules, the interface is similar; you use the `loads` method to obtain a Python object from its JSON representation and the `dumps` method to convert an object into its JSON equivalent.

The previous listing does just this. It defines a variable `j` that contains our JSON, and then obtains a Python object `result` using `json.loads`. Fields in the JSON are accessible as named objects in the resulting Python object. (Note that we can't call our JSON string `json` because it would shadow the definition of the interface to the module.)

To convert to JSON, we use the `json.dumps` method. By default, `dumps` creates a compact machine-readable version of JSON with minimum whitespace; this is best used for over-the-wire transmissions or for storage in a file. When you're debugging your JSON, it helps to pretty-print it with indentation and some whitespace around separators; you can do this using the optional `indent` and `separators` arguments. The `indent` argument indicates the number of spaces that each successive nested object should be indented in the string, and `separators` indicates the separators between each object and between each attribute and value.

See also

For more documentation on the `json` module, see the Python documentation at https://docs.python.org/2/library/json.html.

2
Reading and Writing JSON on the Server

In the previous chapter, we looked at JSON handling in some of the most common client-side environments. In this chapter, we will turn our attention to server-side JSON encoding and decoding. We'll look at recipes on how to do this in the following environments:

- Reading and writing JSON in Clojure
- Reading and writing JSON in F#
- Reading and writing JSON in Node.js
- Reading and writing JSON in PHP
- Reading and writing JSON in Ruby

Some languages, such as C++ and Java, are used on both client-side and server-side; for these, refer to *Chapter 1, Reading and Writing JSON on the Client* (one exception is the discussion of JSON in Node.js because Node.js plays a big role in subsequent chapters of this book).

Reading and writing JSON in Clojure

Clojure is a modern Lisp variant running on top of the Java and Microsoft **Common Language Runtime** (**CLR**) platforms. As such, you can use the facilities we discussed in *Chapter 1, Reading and Writing JSON on the Client*, to convert between JSON and objects in the native runtime, but there's a better way, and that is the Clojure's `data.json` module, available at `https://github.com/clojure/data.json`.

Getting ready

To begin, you need to specify your dependency in the `data.json` module. You can do this with the following dependency in your Leiningen file:

```
[org.clojure/data.json "0.2.5"]
```

If you're using Maven, you'll want this:

```
<dependency>
<groupId>org.clojure</groupId>
<artifactId>data.json</artifactId>
<version>0.2.5</version>
</dependency>
```

 Of course, the version of `data.json` may change between the time I write this and the time you include it in your project as a dependency. Check with the data.json project for the current version.

Finally, you need to include the `data.json` module in your code in a namespace such as `json`:

```
(ns example
  (:require [clojure.data.json :as json]))
```

This makes the implementation of the `data.json` module available through the namespace `json`.

How to do it...

Encoding a Clojure map as JSON is easy, just call `json/write-str`. For example:

```
(json/write-str {:call "KF6GPE",:type "l",:time
"1399371514":lasttime"1418597513",:lat 37.17667,:lng
-122.14650: :result "ok"})
;;=>"{\"call\": \"KF6GPE\", \"type\": \"l\", \"time\":
\"1399371514\", \"lasttime\": \"1418597513\", \"lat\": 37.17667,
\"lng\": -122.14650,\"result\":\"ok\"}"
```

If you've got a stream implementing `java.io.Writer` that you want to write the JSON to, you can also use `json/write`:

```
(json/write {:call "KF6GPE",:type "l", :time
"1399371514":lasttime "1418597513",:lat 37.17667, :lng
-122.14650: result "ok" }  stream)
```

OReading is the opposite of writing and reads JSON into associative arrays that you can process further:

```
(json/read-str "{\"result\":\"ok\"}")
;;=> {"result" "ok"}
```

Also, there's `json/read`, the counterpart of `json/write` that takes a stream from which you can read and return a map of the parsed JSON.

There's more...

These methods all take two optional arguments, a `:key-fn` argument that the module applies to each JSON attribute name, and a `:value-fn` argument that the module applies to attribute values. For example, you can convert JSON to the more traditional Clojure keyword maps using the `:key-fn` keyword, like this:

```
(json/read-str "{\"call\": \"KF6GPE\", \"type\": \"l\", \"time\":
\"1399371514\", \"lasttime\": \"1418597513\", \"lat\": 37.17667,
\"lng\": -122.14650,\"result\":\"ok\"}:key-fn keyword)
;;=> {:call "KF6GPE",:type "l", :time
"1399371514":lasttime "1418597513",:lat 37.17667, :lng
-122.14650: :result "ok"}
```

Alternatively, you can provide a lambda, such as the following one, that converts keys to uppercase:

```
(json/write-str {:result "OK"}
                :key-fn #(.toUpperCase %))
;;=> "{\"RESULT\":"OK"}"
```

Here's a nice example from the `data.json` documentation that uses `:value-fn` to convert ISO dates as strings to Java `Date` objects as you parse the JSON:

```
(defn my-value-reader [key value]
  (if (= key :date)
    (java.sql.Date/valueOf value)
    value))

(json/read-str "{\"result\":\"OK\",\"date\":\"2012-06-02\"}"
                :value-fn my-value-reader
                :key-fn keyword)
;;=> {:result"OK", :date #inst "2012-06-02T04:00:00.000-00:00"}
```

The preceding code does the following:

1. Defines a helper function `my-value-reader` that uses the keyword of the JSON key-value pair to determine its type.

2. Given a JSON key value of `:date`, it treats the value as a string to be passed to the `java.sql.Date` method `valueOf`, which returns a `Date` instance with the value from the string it parses.

3. Calls `json/read-str` to parse some simple JSON consisting of two fields: a `result` field and a `date` field.

4. The JSON parser parses the JSON, converts JSON attribute names to keywords, and uses the value converter we previously defined to convert date values to their `java.sql.Date` representation.

Reading and writing JSON in F#

F# is a language running on the CLR and .NET that excels in functional and object-oriented programming tasks. Because it's on top of .NET, you can use third-party libraries such as `Json.NET` (mentioned in *Chapter 1, Reading and Writing JSON on the Client*) to convert between JSON and CLR objects. However, there's a better way: the open source library F# Data, which creates native data type providers to process data in a number of different structured formats, including JSON.

Getting ready

Begin by getting a copy of the library, available at `https://github.com/fsharp/FSharp.Data`. Once you download it, you'll need to build it; you can do this by running the `build.cmd` build batch file that comes with the distribution (for details, see the F# Data website). Alternatively, you can find the same package on NuGet, by choosing **Manage NuGet Packages** from the **Projects** menu and searching for F# Data. Once you find it, click on **Install**. I prefer using NuGet because it automatically adds the `FSharp.Data` assembly to your project, and saves you the hassle of building the sources on your own. On the other hand, the source distribution makes documentation you can read offline, which can be handy, too.

Once you have the F# Data, you simply need to open it in the source files where you're going to use it with the open directive, like this:

```
open FSharp.Data
```

How to do it...

Here's a bit of sample code that converts between some JSON and an F# object, and then makes a new bit of JSON from another F# object:

```
open FSharp.Data

type Json = JsonProvider<""" { "result":"" } """>
let result = Json.Parse(""" { "result":"OK" } """)
let newJson = Json.Root( result = "FAIL")

[<EntryPoint>]
let main argv =
    printfn "%A" result.Result
    printfn "%A" newJson
    printfn "Done"
```

Let's see how it works.

How it works...

First, it's important to remember that F# is strongly typed and infers types from data. Understanding this is crucial to understand how the F# Data library works. Unlike the examples we've seen in past sections, where converters map JSON to key-value pairs, the F# Data library infers a whole data type from the JSON you present it with. In many ways, this is the best of both the dynamic collection-oriented approach, that other converters take to converting JSON, and the type-safe approaches that I'll show you in *Chapter 7, Using JSON in a Type-safe Manner*. This is because you don't have to laboriously craft class representations for the JSON you're parsing, and you get all the advantages of compile-time type safety in the code you write. Even better, the classes F# Data construct are all Intellisense-aware, so you get tooltip hints and name completion right in the editor!

Let's look at the previous example piece by piece and see what it does:

```
open FSharp.Data
```

The first line makes the F# Data classes available to your program. Among other things, this defines the `JsonProvider` class, which creates F# types from sources of JSON:

```
type Json= JsonProvider<""" { "result":"" } """>
```

This line defines a new F# type, `Json`, with fields and field types inferred from the JSON you provide. Under the hood, this does a lot: it infers member names, the types of members, and even handles things such as mixed numeric values (say that you have an array with both integers and floating-point numbers, it correctly infers the type as numeric so you can represent either), as well as complex records and optional fields.

You can pass one of the following three things to `JsonProvider`:

1. A string containing JSON. This is the simplest case.
2. A path to a file containing JSON. The library will open the file and read the contents and perform the type inference on the contents, and then return a type capable of representing the JSON in the file.
3. A URL. The library will fetch the document at the URL, parse the JSON, and then do the same type inference on the contents, returning a type that represents the JSON at the URL.

The next line parses a single JSON document, as follows:

```
let result = Json.Parse(""" { "result":"OK" } """)
```

This at first may seem a little weird: why are we passing JSON to both the `JsonProvider` and `Parse` methods? Recall that `JsonProvider` makes a type from the JSON you provide. In other words, it doesn't parse the JSON for its values, but for the types of data it represents in order to make a class that can model the JSON document itself. This is very important; to the `JsonProvider`, you'll want to pass a representative JSON document that has the fields and values common across all the JSON documents of a particular type that your application is likely to encounter. You'll pass a specific JSON document (say, a web service result) to the `Parse` method of the class that `JsonProvider` creates. In turn, `Parse` returns an instance of the class on which you invoked `Parse`.

You can now access the fields in the instance of the class `Parse` returns; for example, later, I will print the value of `result.Result` in my application's `main` function.

To create JSON, you need an instance of the type modeling the data you want to serialize. In the next line, we use the `Json` type we just created to create a new JSON string:

```
let newJson = Json.Root( result = "FAIL")
```

This creates an instance of the `Json` type with the result field set to the string `FAIL`, and then serializes that instance into a new string.

Finally, the remainder of the program is our program's entry point, and just prints the parsed object and the created JSON.

There's more...

The F# Data library supports a lot more than just JSON; it also supports **Comma Separated Values** (**CSV**), HTML, and XML. It's an excellent library for doing all kinds of structured data access, and if you're working in F#, it's definitely something to become more familiar with.

Reading and writing JSON with Node.js

Node.js is a JavaScript environment for server-side programming based on the same high-performance JavaScript runtime Google built for Chrome, backed by Joyent. Its high performing and asynchronous programming model makes it an excellent environment for custom web servers and it's used by major companies, including Walmart, in production settings.

Getting ready

Because we'll use Node.js in the next two chapters as well, it's worth pointing out to you how to download and install it, even if your daily server environment is something more like Apache or Microsoft IIS. You'll need to go to `http://www.nodejs.org/` and download the installer from the front page. This will install all you need to run Node.js and npm, the package manager used by Node.js.

 After installing on Windows, I had to reboot to get the Windows shell to correctly find the node and npm commands that the Node.js installer installed.

Once you get Node.js installed, we can test the installation by bringing up a simple HTTP server in Node.js. To do this, put the following code in a file called `example.js`:

```
var http = require('http');
http.createServer(function(req, res) {
    res.writeHead(200, {'Content-Type': 'text/plain'});
    res.end('Hello world\n');
}).listen(1337, 'localhost');
console.log('Server running at http://localhost:1337');
```

This code loads Node.js's `http` module, and then creates a Web server bound to the port `1337` running on your local machine. You can run it by entering the following command at a command prompt in the same directory as the file you created:

```
node example.js
```

Once you do so, point your browser to the URL `http://localhost:1337/`. If everything's successful, you should see the message "Hello world" in your web browser.

 You may need to tell your system firewall to enable access to ports being served by the `node` command.

How to do it...

Since Node.js uses Chrome's V8 JavaScript engine, working with JSON is the same with Node.js as it is in Chrome. The JavaScript runtime defines the `JSON` object, which provides a JSON parser and serializer for you.

To parse JSON, all you need to do is invoke the `JSON.parse` method, like this:

```
var json = '{ "call":"KF6GPE","type":"l","time":
"1399371514","lasttime":"1418597513","lat": 37.17667,"lng":
-122.14650,"result" : "ok" }';
var object = JSON.parse(json);
```

This parses the JSON, returning the JavaScript object containing the data, which we assigned here to the variable object.

Of course, you can do the opposite, using `JSON.stringify`, like this:

```
var object = {
call:"KF6GPE",
type:"l",
time:"1399371514",
lasttime:"1418597513",
lat:37.17667,
lng:-122.14650,
result: "ok"
};

var json = JSON.stringify(object);
```

See also

For more on parsing and creating JSON in JavaScript, see *Reading and Writing JSON in JavaScript* in *Chapter 1, Reading and Writing JSON on the Client.*

Reading and writing JSON in PHP

PHP is a popular server-side scripting environment easily integrated with the Apache and Microsoft IIS web servers. It has native support for simple JSON encoding and decoding.

How to do it...

PHP provides two functions, `json_encode` and `json_decode`, to encode and decode JSON respectively.

You can pass primitive types or user-defined classes to `json_encode` and it returns a string containing the JSON representing the object. For example:

```
$result = array(
"call" =>"KF6GPE",
"type" =>"1",
"time" =>"1399371514",
"lasttime" =>"1418597513",
"lat" =>37.17667,
"lng" =>-122.14650,
"result" =>"ok");
$json = json_encode($result);
```

This creates a string `$json` containing the JSON representation of our associative array.

The `json_encode` function takes an optional second argument, which lets you specify arguments to the encoder. The arguments are flags, so you combine them with the binary or | operator. You can pass a combination of the following flags:

▸   `JSON_FORCE_OBJECT`: This flag forces the encoder to encode the JSON as an object.

▸   `JSON_NUMERIC_CHECK`: This flag checks the contents of each string in the incoming structure and if it contains a number, converts the string to a number before encoding it.

▸   `JSON_PRETTY_PRINT`: This flag formats the JSON for easier reading by humans (don't do this in production, as it makes the JSON bigger)

▸   `JSON_UNESCAPED_SLASHES`: This flag instructs the encoder to not escape slash characters.

Finally, you can pass a third argument, which specifies the depth to which the encoder should walk the expression when encoding the value you pass.

The complement of `json_encode` is `json_decode`, which takes the JSON to decode, and a set of optional arguments. Its simplest use might be something like this:

```
$json = '{ "call":"KF6GPE","type":"1","time":
"1399371514","lasttime":"1418597513","lat": 37.17667,"lng":
-122.14650,"result" : "ok" }';
$result = json_decode($json);
```

The `json_decode` function takes up to three optional arguments:

▸   The first argument, when true, specifies that the result should be returned in an associative array rather than an object of type `stdClass`.

▸   The second argument specifies an optional recursion depth to determine how deep into the JSON the parser should parse.

- ▶ The third argument may be the option `JSON_BIGINT_AS_STRING`, which when set indicates that integers that overflow the integer values should be returned as strings, not cast to floating-point numbers (which may lose precision).

These functions return `true` on success or `false` on error; you can determine the cause of the last error using JSON by examining the return value of `json_last_error`.

Reading and writing JSON in Ruby

Ruby provides the `json` gem for JSON handling. In earlier versions of Ruby, you have to install this gem yourself; it's part of the base installation from Ruby 1.9.2 and onwards.

Getting ready

If you're running an earlier version of Ruby than Ruby 1.9.2, first install the gem with the following command:

gem install json

Note that Ruby's implementation is in C, so installing the gem may require a C compiler. If you don't have one installed on your system, you can install the pure Ruby implementation of the gem using the following command:

gem install json_pure

Regardless of whether you need to install the gem or not, you'll need to include it in your code. To do this, include both `rubygems` and `json` or **json/pure**, depending on which gem you installed; do this using `require`, like this:

```
require 'rubygems'
require 'json'
```

The preceding code handles the former case, while the following code handles the latter:

```
require 'rubygems'
require 'json/pure'
```

How to do it...

The gem defines the JSON object, which includes the methods `parse` and `generate`, which serialize and deserialize JSON respectively. Using them is what you'd expect by now. Create an object or some JSON, invoke the appropriate function, and look at the results. For example, to create some JSON using JSON.generate, you can execute the following:

```
require 'rubygems'
require 'json'
```

```
object = {
"call" =>"KF6GPE",
"type" =>"l",
"time" =>"1399371514",
"lasttime" =>"1418597513",
"lat" => 37.17667,
"lng" => -122.14650,
"result" =>"ok"
}
json = JSON.generate(object)
```

This includes the necessary modules, creates an associative array with a single field, and then serializes it to JSON.

Deserializing works the same way:

```
require 'rubygems'
require 'json'
json = '{ "call":"KF6GPE","type":"l","time":
"1399371514","lasttime":"1418597513","lat": 37.17667,"lng":
-122.14650,"result" : "ok" }'
object = JSON.parse(object)
```

The parse function can take an optional second argument, a hash with the following keys, indicating options to the parser:

- ▸ `max_nesting` indicates the maximum depth of nesting allowed in the parsed data structures. It defaults to 19 or you can disable the nesting depth checking by passing `:max_nesting => false`.

- ▸ `allow_nan`, which if set to true, allows NaN, Infinity, and -Infinity in defiance of RFC 4627 to be parsed.

- ▸ `symbolize_names`, which when true, returns symbols for the attribute names in a JSON object; otherwise, strings are returned (strings are the default).

See also

Documentation for the JSON Ruby gem is available on the Web at
`http://flori.github.io/json/doc/index.html`.

3
Using JSON in Simple AJAX Applications

In this chapter, we'll look at the part that JSON plays in asynchronous JavaScript and XML (AJAX) applications that provide better responsiveness than older web pages by dynamically loading bits of a web page on demand.

In this chapter, you'll find the following recipes:

- ▶ Creating an `XMLHttpRequest` object
- ▶ Making an asynchronous request for data
- ▶ Sending JSON to your web server
- ▶ Accepting JSON using Node.js
- ▶ Getting the progress of an asynchronous request
- ▶ Parsing the returned JSON
- ▶ Issuing a web service request using Node.js

Introduction

AJAX is a set of web development techniques used on the client side of web development to create asynchronous web applications—web pages that can fetch their content from different servers, once the base content has been loaded. The "X" in AJAX stands for XML, but today's AJAX applications typically use JSON to encapsulate data between the client and server.

The underpinning components of AJAX are actually quite old, dating back to an ActiveX component in Internet Explorer introduced by Microsoft back in 1998.

However, the technique really gained widespread traction by 2005, when *Jesse Garrett* wrote his article titled *Ajax: A New Approach to Web Applications*. In April of 2006, the World Wide Web Consortium released the first draft standard for the `XMLHttpRequest` object, which is the underlying object powering all of today's AJAX applications in modern browsers.

In this chapter, we'll build a simple AJAX application that returns the latitude and longitude of an amateur radio station reported through the **Automated Packet Reporting System** (**APRS**) network as cached by `http://www.aprs.fi/`, a popular website in the amateur radio community. We'll build the client side using HTML and JavaScript for Google Chrome and Internet Explorer, and build the server side using Node.js.

To begin, be sure you installed Node.js as instructed in *Chapter 2, Reading and Writing JSON on the Server*, in the section *Reading and writing JSON with Node.js*. You'll also need to install the request module of Node.js. Do this by running `npm install request` at a command prompt once you've installed Node.js.

Setting up the server

We'll start with a bare-bones server. Make a directory for your node applications and save the following to `json-encoder.js`:

```
var http = require('http');
var fs = require('fs');
var url = require('url');

http.createServer(function(req, res) {
if (req.method == 'POST') {
  console.log('POST');
  var body = '';
  req.on('data', function(data) {
    body += data;
  });
  req.on('end', function() {
    res.writeHead(200,
      {'Content-Type': 'application/json'});
    res.end("null");
    });
  }
  elseif (req.method == 'GET')
  {
    console.log('GET');
    var urlParts = url.parse(req.url);
    if (urlParts.pathname == "/favicon.ico")
```

```
    {
      res.end("");
      return;
    }

    res.writeHead(200, {'Content-Type': 'text/plain'});

    var html = fs.readFileSync('./public' + urlParts.pathname);
    res.writeHead(200, {'Content-Type': 'text/html'});
    res.end(html);
    return;
  }
}).listen(1337, 'localhost');
console.log('Server running at http://127.0.0.1:1337');
```

This code handles two kinds of HTTP requests: POST requests and GET requests. It begins by allocating `http`, `filesystem`, and `url` manipulation objects, and then registers an HTTP server on port `1337` of the localhost. Its server switches on the request type. For POST requests, it presently returns an empty JSON body, ignoring its incoming content. For GET requests, it attempts to load the file indicated in the URL out of the `public` subdirectory below the current working directory and return it to the client as an HTML document. If the incoming request is for a favicon, it ignores the request.

This server is crude but adequate for our purposes. If you're interested in learning more about Node.js, you might want to extend it for the following purposes:

▸ Correctly determine the MIME type of the documents it returns, and send the appropriate Content-Type header based on the document MIME type.

▸ Not throw an exception and kill the server if a given document isn't found, returning a 404 page not found error instead.

We'll extend the server-side JavaScript throughout this chapter.

Setting up the client page

Make a subdirectory inside `json-encoder.js` and call it `public`. In this directory, create an HTML file containing the following HTML and name it `json-example.html`:

```
<!DOCTYPE html>
<html>
<head>

</head>
<body onload="doAjax()">
```

```
<p>Hello world</p>
<p>
<div id="debug"></div>
</p>
<p>
<div id="json"></div>
</p>
<p>
<div id="result"></div>
</p>

<p>Powered by <a href="http://www.aprs.fi">aprs.fi</a></p>

<script type="text/javascript">
var debug = document.getElementById('debug');

function doAjax() {
  document.getElementById("result").innerHTML =
    "loaded... executing.";
}
</script>
</body>
</html>
```

This is a simple HTML document with three `div` tags we'll populate with data from the asynchronous requests: `debug` to show debug messages; `json` to show the raw JSON; and `result` to show the actual result, which will show some formatted data from the JavaScript object obtained by parsing the JSON. There's one script at the bottom of the page, `doAjax`, which the browser invokes after loading all the HTML through the `onload` attribute of the body tag.

Loading the web page in Chrome with the developer's tools active, you should see something like this:

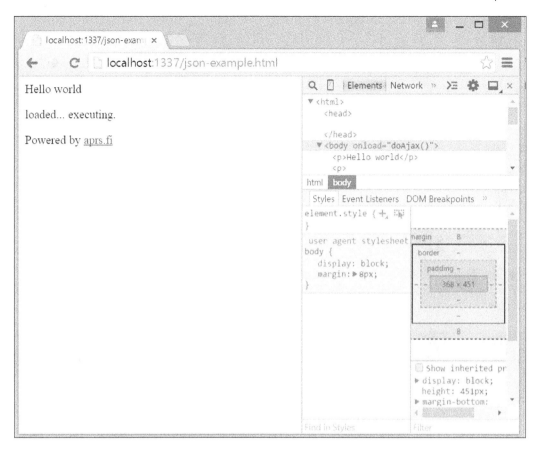

We'll extend the HTML throughout this chapter.

Creating an XMLHttpRequest object

All modern web browsers provide an `XMLHttpRequest` class you can instantiate in your code, which you can use to issue asynchronous calls to obtain content over HTTP. You'll create one or more of these in your client-side JavaScript using the `new` operator.

How to do it...

You'll want to create an instance of this class early on in your JavaScript after the page loads, as shown in the following code:

```
function doAjax() {
var xmlhttp;
```

```
if (window.XMLHttpRequest)
  {
    // code for IE7+, Firefox, Chrome, Opera, Safari
    xmlhttp=new XMLHttpRequest();
  }
}
```

How it works...

The preceding code tests the root-level JavaScript `window` object for the `XMLHttpRequest` class, and if the browser defines the class, creates an instance of the class for us to use in the making of asynchronous requests.

See also

If you're working with a very old version of Internet Explorer, you may need to use a `Microsoft.XMLHTTP` ActiveX object. In which case, the test for `window.XMLHttpRequest` will fail.

Making an asynchronous request for data

You use the instance of the `XMLHttpRequest` class you created to request data. You can request data using any HTTP method; typically you'll use GET or POST. GET is good if you don't need to pass any arguments, or if the arguments are encoded in the service URL; POST is necessary if you're going to post JSON to the server as arguments for your server-side script.

How to do it...

Continuing to enhance our client page script's `doAjax` function, here's how to issue an asynchronous request, modifying the previous example:

```
function doAjax() {
  var xmlhttp;
  if (window.XMLHttpRequest)
  {
    // code for IE7+, Firefox, Chrome, Opera, Safari
    xmlhttp=newXMLHttpRequest();

    xmlhttp.open("POST","/", true);
    xmlhttp.send("");
  }
}
```

How it works...

The `XMLHttpRequest` class has two methods you use to make a request: `open` and `send`. You use the `open` method to start the process of issuing the request, and the `send` method if you need to send data (say, with a `POST` request) for the server to process.

The `open` method takes three arguments: the HTTP method, the URL (relative to the page containing the script), and a Boolean indicating whether the request should be synchronous (indicated by the value `false`) or asynchronous (indicated by the value `true`). In the preceding code, we submit a `POST` request to the web server's root and request the browser to handle the request asynchronously, so the page will be rendered and the user can interact with the page.

The `send` method takes a single argument, a string containing the data you'd like to send to the server. In this example, we're not sending anything; we'll use this method to send the JSON for our argument.

See also

This recipe is closely related to the next, *Sending JSON to your web server*, in which we actually create a JavaScript object, stringify it, and send it using the `send` method.

Sending JSON to your web server

Some AJAX requests just need to get data at a URL. This is the case when the server updates an object for all clients, or when the URL for an object uniquely identifies the object (common when you design a service using **Representational State Transfer** (**REST**)). Other times, you may want to pass JavaScript data to the server, such as when you have a complex query you'd like the server to process. To do this, create your JavaScript object, then stringify it and pass the string containing the JSON to the `XMLHttpRequest` object's `send` method.

How to do it...

Omitting the code that creates an `XMLHttpRequest` object, you send JSON to a server with the following code:

```
function doAjax() {
  // … create XMLHTTPObject as before

    var request = {
    call: "kf6gpe-7"
  };

  xmlhttp.open("POST","/", true);
```

```
xmlhttp.setRequestHeader("Content-Type","application/json");
xmlhttp.send(JSON.stringify(request));
}
```

Note that we're using an HTTP POST request here, which submits the JSON document to the server as an HTTP object body.

How it works...

This code creates a JavaScript object request that has a single field: call. The call field's value is set to the station we're looking for and the server will use it when it processes the request.

When you pass data to the server, you should correctly set the Content-Type header, which HTTP uses to indicate to the server the type of the data being carried. The MIME type for JSON is application/json; however, some web application developers have chosen alternate representations, such as text/x-json, text/x-javascript, text/javascript, or application/x-javascript. You should use application/json unless you have a compelling reason (think legacy code you can't fix on a server). You specify the content type by setting a request header using the setRequestHeader method. This method takes two arguments: the name of the header to set and its value. Note that header names are case sensitive!

Once you set the request header, the final thing to do is call send and pass the stringified JavaScript object. We do this in the last line of the preceding example.

Accepting JSON using Node.js

Different web server systems accept data posted by a client in different ways. That being said, in most cases, you read the data piecewise as it comes in from the client and once the POST request finishes, process it as a batch. Here's how to do it with Node.js.

How to do it...

In our case, we accept JSON submitted from the client via HTTP POST requests. To do this, we need to read the data from the client, aggregate it in a string, and when all of the data arrives at the server, convert the data from a JSON string to a JavaScript object. In json-encoder, js, we modify it to read as the following:

```
// … beginning of script is the same as in the introduction
if (req.method == 'POST') {
  console.log('POST');
  var body = '';
  req.on('data', function(data) {
    body += data;
  });
```

```
      req.on('end', function() {
      var json = JSON.parse(body);
      json.result = 'OK';
      res.writeHead(200,
        {'Content-Type': 'application/json'});

      res.end(JSON.stringify(json));
    });
  }
  // and script continues with the GET if statement and code
```

How it works...

The preceding code extends the server-side Node.js script we saw in this chapter's introduction. The code begins by testing for the POST request method. If we get a POST request, we create an empty string `body` to contain the body of the request. Node.js is event-driven; to read data from the POST request, we add a `'data'` event handler to the request, which concatenates newly-read data to the value referred to by the variable `body`.

At some point, the POST request concludes, which causes the request to raise the `'end'` event. We register an event handler for this event, which uses JSON.parse to parse the incoming JSON. Then, we set an additional field in the resulting object, the result field, giving it a value of `'OK'`. Finally, we write the Content-Type header and then the JSON representing the object to the client using the `writeHead` and `end` methods respectively.

See also

As suggested in the introduction, how you read posted data on your server depends a lot on the server environment and server-side scripting language. If you haven't done this before, a quick trip to a search engine such as Bing or Google is in order. Once you do so, be prepared to take the resulting string data and convert it to an object in your server-side scripting language using one of the recipes from *Chapter 2, Reading and Writing JSON on the Server*.

Getting the progress of an asynchronous request

Our request is pretty lightweight but that's not always going to be the case in your application. Moreover, progressing is especially important in mobile web applications, where the mobile device may move in and out of network coverage and suffer temporary network outages. A robust application will test progress status and errors and retry important requests.

The `XMLHttpRequest` object provides events for it to notify you about the progress of a pending request. These events are as follows:

- ▸ `load`: This event executes immediately after you open a connection.
- ▸ `loadstart`: This event executes as a load first starts.
- ▸ `progress`: This event executes periodically as the load takes place.
- ▸ `error`: This event executes in the event of a network error.
- ▸ `abort`: This event executes in the event that the network transaction is aborted (such as the user navigating away from the page issuing the request).

How to do it...

For each of these events, you'll want to register a function that handles the event in some way. For example, the `error` handler should notify the user that an error occurs, while the `abort` handler should clean up any client-side data that is left lingering in the event of an abandoned request.

Here's an example of how to do this, which reports debugging information for each of these events; this would go in the `<script>` tag at the bottom of our example HTML:

```
// Add the following functions to the script in the HTML...
function progress(evt){
   debug.innerHTML += "'progress' called...<...<br/>";/>";
}

function abort(evt){
   debug.innerHTML += "'abort' called...<br />";
}

function error(evt){
   debug.innerHTML += "'error' called...<br />";
}

function load(evt){
   debug.innerHTML += "'load' called...<br />";
}

function loadstart(evt){
   debug.innerHTML += "'loadstart' called<br />;
}

function doAjax() {
   // create xmlhttp object as usual
```

```
var request = {
  call: "kf6gpe-7"
};

xmlhttp.addEventListener("loadstart", loadstart, false);
xmlhttp.addEventListener("progress", progress, false);
xmlhttp.addEventListener("load", load, false);
xmlhttp.addEventListener("abort", abort, false);
xmlhttp.addEventListener("error", error, false);

// issue request in the usual way…
}
```

How it works...

The `XMLHttpRequest` object offers the `addEventListener` method, which you use to register functions the object should invoke when particular events occur. To this method, you pass the name of the event, the function (or a closure) to invoke on the event, and whether the registered function should capture the event or not (usually not). In the preceding example, we invoke that method for each of the events, passing the function that we wrote to handle the event. Each of our functions just logs the fact that the event was received in the debug div in our HTML content.

There's more...

The `XMLHttpResult` object defines an attribute, `onreadystatechange`, to which you can assign a function that the object will invoke periodically as the request runs. The next recipe, *Parsing the returned JSON*, describes how to use this to monitor the status of a request.

The behavior of these events varies from browser to browser, and worse, from browser version to browser version. For example, early versions of Microsoft Internet Explorer (prior to Version 9) don't support these events at all. You should take a lowest-common-denominator approach to handle these events if your web application is to run on multiple browsers, especially if they're different versions.

See also

Because the support for these events varies by browser and browser version, this is another area where using a JavaScript framework such as jQuery or AngularJS can really help. These frameworks abstract away specific browser differences. *Chapter 4, Using JSON in AJAX Applications with jQuery and AngularJS,* discusses using these frameworks for AJAX.

See *Getting the progress of an asynchronous request using jQuery* and *Getting the progress of an asynchronous request using AngularJS* in *Chapter 4, Using JSON in AJAX Applications with jQuery and AngularJS*, for browser-independent ways to respond to these events.

Parsing the returned JSON

Once the server returns the result, you need a way to get that result from the XMLHttpRequest object and convert the result from a string to a JavaScript object.

How to do it...

The XMLHttpRequest object defines the onreadystatechange attribute to which you assign a function that is called periodically throughout the lifespan of a request. Here's our doAjax function in its entirety, including a function assigned to this attribute to monitor the request for completion:

```
function doAjax() {
  var xmlhttp;
  xmlhttp = new XMLHttpRequest();

  var request = {
    call: "kf6gpe-7"
  };

  xmlhttp.addEventListener("loadstart", loadstart, false);
  xmlhttp.addEventListener("progress", progress, false);
  xmlhttp.addEventListener("load", load, false);
  xmlhttp.addEventListener("abort", abort, false);
  xmlhttp.addEventListener("error", error, false);

  xmlhttp.onreadystatechange = function() {
    if (xmlhttp.readyState == 4 &&xmlhttp.status == 200)
    {
      var result = JSON.parse(xmlhttp.responseText);
      document.getElementById("json").innerHTML =
        xmlhttp.responseText;
      document.getElementById("result").innerHTML = result.call + ":"
+ result.lat + ", " + result.lng;
    }
  };

  xmlhttp.open("POST","/", true);
```

```
xmlhttp.setRequestHeader("Content-type","application/json");
xmlhttp.send(JSON.stringify(request));
}
```

How it works...

After adding the various event listeners, we assign a function to the `onreadystatechange` attribute. This function is called as the state of the request object changes; at each invocation, we test the `readyState` field of the request object and its status. The `readyState` field indicates the state of the request; we're interested in state 4, which indicates that the request is complete. Once complete, we can find the HTTP status of the request in the status field of the request; the HTTP status code 200 indicates a normal successful status in reading content from the server.

Once we get `readyState` of 4 and a HTTP status of 200, we define a new variable `result` as the object returned by parsing the JSON returned by the server, available from the request's `responseText` field. You can do whatever you want with the resulting object; we copy the JSON to `jsondiv` so you can see the JSON and read a few fields of the JavaScript object when we create the contents of `resultdiv`.

There's more...

The `XMLHttpRequest` class defines the following ready states:

- 0 indicates that the request has not been initialized
- 1 indicates that the request has been set up
- 2 indicates that the request has been sent
- 3 indicates that the request is in progress
- 4 indicates that the request is complete

In practice, you should usually use only the last value and use events for other progress reporting.

HTTP result codes are defined in the HTTP request for comment, Internet RFC 2616; the section you'd be interested in for this purpose is at `http://www.w3.org/Protocols/rfc2616/rfc2616-sec10.html`. The 200 series of results indicate a successful transaction; how you handle the other notifications will depend on the business logic for your web application.

The final Node.js server looks like this:

```
var http = require('http');
var fs = require('fs');
var url = require('url');
```

```
      var request = require("request");

      console.log("Starting");

      http.createServer(function(req, res) {
        if (req.method == 'POST') {
          console.log('POST');
          var body = '';
          req.on('data', function(data) {
            body += data;
          });
          req.on('end', function() {
            var json = JSON.parse(body);
            var apiKey = "<<key>>";
            var serviceUrl = "http://api.aprs.fi/api/get?name=" +
            json.call + "&what=loc&apikey=" + apiKey + "&format=json";
            request(serviceUrl, function(error, response, body) {
              var bodyObject = JSON.parse(body);
              if (bodyObject.entries.length>0)
              {
                json.call = bodyObject.entries[0].name;
                json.lat = bodyObject.entries[0].lat;
                json.lng = bodyObject.entries[0].lng;
                json.result = "OK";
              }
              else
              {
                json.result = "ERROR";
              }
              res.writeHead(200, {'Content-Type': 'application/json'});
              res.end(JSON.stringify(json));
            });
          });
        }
        elseif (req.method == 'GET')
        {
          console.log('GET');
          var urlParts = url.parse(req.url);
          if (urlParts.pathname == "/favicon.ico")
          {
            res.end("");
            return;
          }
          res.writeHead(200, {'Content-Type': 'text/plain'});
```

```
    var html = fs.readFileSync('./public' + urlParts.pathname);
    res.writeHead(200, {'Content-Type': 'text/html'});
    res.end(html);
    return;
  }
}).listen(1337, 'localhost');
console.log('Server running at http://localhost:1337');
```

Issuing a web service request using Node.js

So far, our server doesn't do much in response to a POST request; all it does is say "OK" and return the client's JSON back to the client. Typically, your server will need to do something with the JSON you provide, that is, make a web or database query, for example, or perform a computation. Our example queries the web service JSON endpoint at http://www.aprs.fi/, which lets you see how you can make a server-to-server web service request using Node.js.

Getting ready

If you want to run the example for yourself, you'll first need to go to http://www.aprs.fi, register for an account, and obtain an API key. Follow the links on the page to do this, and substitute your API key for the text "-key-" in the example that follows.

How to do it...

Our Node.js code will construct a URL with the identifier of the station we're interested in and our API key, and issue an additional HTTP request on behalf of the client. It looks like this:

```
var request = require('server');

///...

if (req.method == 'POST') {
  console.log('POST');
  var body = '';
  req.on('data', function(data) {
    body += data;
  });
  req.on('end', function() {
    var json = JSON.parse(body);
    var apiKey = "-key-";
    var serviceUrl = "http://api.aprs.fi/api/get?name=" +
                     json.call +
                     "&what=loc&apikey=" + apiKey +
```

```
                        "&format=json";

    request(serviceUrl, function(error, response, body) {
      var bodyObject = JSON.parse(body);
      if (bodyObject.entries.length>0)
      {
        json.call = bodyObject.entries[0].name;
        json.lat = bodyObject.entries[0].lat;
        json.lng = bodyObject.entries[0].lng;
        json.result = "OK";
      }
      else
      {
        json.result = "ERROR";
      }
      res.writeHead(200,
        {'Content-Type': 'application/json'});

      res.end(JSON.stringify(json));
    });
  });
}
elseif (req.method == 'GET')
{
  // …Original GET handling code here…
}
}).listen(1337, 'localhost');
console.log('Server running at http://127.0.0.1:1337');
```

How it works...

After converting the client JSON to a JavaScript object, the code creates a URL for our web request consisting of the request station identifier, API key, and the fact that we'd like JSON for the result. We then use the `request` method to issue a simple GET request to that URL, passing a function that Node.js will invoke when the request succeeds.

Node.js invokes our callback function with an indicator of an error, a response object with fields containing the details of the HTTP response, and the body returned by the request. In this example, we assume success for brevity, and convert the resulting body from JSON to a JavaScript object using `JSON.parse`. The resulting object is a JavaScript object similar to what you saw in *Chapter 1, Reading and Writing JSON on the Client*, in the *Introduction* section. It has an entries array which has zero or more records indicating the location of each station in the record's `lat` and `lng` fields. We extract the first returned result and copy the relevant data to the JavaScript object we'll return to the original client.

There's more...

Most server-side frameworks provide various ways to modify the semantics of a web service request, including specifying headers and the HTTP method to use when issuing the request. Node.js's request module is no different.

First, the request method can take a JavaScript object instead of a URL with a number of fields that let you customize the request. If you pass an object, you should put the URL to which the request should be made in the URI or URL attributes. You can also specify the following:

- The HTTP method to use, which is passed in the method parameter
- The HTTP headers to send, which are passed as a JavaScript object with attribute-value pairs for each header in the attribute headers
- A body to pass to the client for `PATCH`, `POST`, and `PUT` method requests, in the body attribute
- A timeout indicating how long to wait in milliseconds in the timeout attribute
- Whether or not to gzip the response, indicated by setting the gzip attribute to `true`

Other options are available as well. See the Node.js documentation for details at `https://nodejs.org/api/index.html`.

See also

The Node.js request module has its documentation on GitHub at `https://github.com/request/request`

4

Using JSON in AJAX Applications with jQuery and AngularJS

In this chapter, we'll look at the part that JSON plays in asynchronous JavaScript and XML (AJAX) applications that provide better responsiveness than older web pages by dynamically loading bits of a web page on demand. In this chapter, you'll find the following recipes:

- ▸ Adding a dependency to jQuery to your web page
- ▸ Requesting JSON content using jQuery
- ▸ Sending JSON to your web server using jQuery
- ▸ Getting the progress of a request using jQuery
- ▸ Parsing the returned JSON using jQuery
- ▸ Adding a dependency to AngularJS to your web page
- ▸ Requesting JSON content using AngularJS
- ▸ Sending JSON to your web server using AngularJS
- ▸ Getting the progress of a request using AngularJS
- ▸ Parsing the returned JSON using AngularJS

Introduction

In the last chapter, you saw recipes that showed you how to use `XMLHttpRequest` to make AJAX requests that exchanged JSON. In practice, handling all of the special cases in different browsers makes this a pesky, error-prone job. Fortunately, most client-side JavaScript frameworks wrap this object for you, giving you a browser-independent way to do the same thing. Often, the interface is easier to use too—as you'll soon see, in the case of AngularJS, you don't need to do anything special to move objects back and forth using JSON; the framework even takes care of serializing and deserializing the JSON for you!

Both AngularJS and jQuery are client-side JavaScript frameworks that make developing web applications easier. jQuery was one of the first and is probably the most widely adopted framework; AngularJS is newer and has the additional advantage of providing you with the ability to structure your code using the **model-view-controller** (**MVC**) paradigm.

MVC is a design pattern that dates back decades, originally introduced as a part of Smalltalk in the 1970s. This pattern divides your code into three distinct segments: the model, which contains the data your user wants to manipulate, the view, which shows the contents of the model, and the controller, which accepts events and changes the model in response to the accepted events.

In this chapter, we will use the server in Node.js that we based last chapter's recipes on, with an extension to support serving client-side JavaScript as well as HTML. Here's the code for this, broken down step by step:

```
var http = require('http');
var fs = require('fs');
var url = require('url');
var request = require("request");
```

These four lines include the interfaces our server needs—the modules to handle the HTTP server module, the file system module, the URL parsing module, and a simple module to make HTTP requests.

Next, we log that the server starts and create an HTTP server that accepts all requests with a single function callback:

```
console.log("Starting");
http.createServer(function(req, res) {
```

Our server handles two kinds of requests: POST requests and GET requests. The POST request handler needs to read the incoming data that's been posted to the server, which we do by concatenating it with an originally empty body buffer:

```
if (req.method == 'POST') {
  console.log('POST');
  var body = '';
  req.on('data', function(data) {
    body += data;
  });
```

We register a function that Node.js calls back when the HTTP post finishes, which parses the JSON and makes a GET request to the remote server for our data, simulating what a middleware server might do:

```
req.on('end', function() {
  var json = JSON.parse(body);

  var apiKey = " --- api key here --- ";
  var serviceUrl = "http://api.aprs.fi/api/get?name=" +
    json.call + "&what=loc&apikey=" + apiKey + "&format=json";
```

This request itself has a callback, which parses the incoming JSON from the remote server, looks for the first element of the array in the result entries attribute, and constructs a JSON object to return to the web client. If we don't get a valid response, we set an error value so the client can do something with the error. We return this by converting the JavaScript object to JSON and writing it to the client:

```
    request(serviceUrl, function(error, response, body) {
      var bodyObject = JSON.parse(body);
      if (bodyObject.entries.length>0)
      {
        json.call = bodyObject.entries[0].name;
        json.lat = bodyObject.entries[0].lat;
        json.lng = bodyObject.entries[0].lng;
        json.result = "OK";
      }
      else
      {
        json.result = "ERROR";
      }
      res.writeHead(200, {'Content-Type': 'application/json'});
      res.end(JSON.stringify(json));
    });
  });
}
```

If it's not a POST request we're handling, it might be a GET request. Here's the new code from the last chapter. We need to determine whether the incoming URL indicates that the content to be fetched is an HTML file (whose suffix is .html or .htm) or a JavaScript file (whose suffix is .js). First, we see whether we're getting a request for a favicon; Chrome always does this, and we just return an empty object body. Assuming that it's not a favicon being requested, we check the incoming URL to see how it ends, so we can write the appropriate Content-Type header (either text/html or application/json). If it's neither of those, we assume plaintext and send a text/plain Content-Type header:

```
else if (req.method == 'GET')
{
  console.log('GET');
  var urlParts = url.parse(req.url);
  if (urlParts.pathname == "/favicon.ico")
  {
    res.end("");
    return;
  }

  if (urlParts.pathname.lastIndexOf(".html") ==
        urlParts.pathname.length - 5 ||
      urlParts.pathname.lastIndexOf(".htm") ==
        urlParts.pathname.length - 4)
  {
    res.writeHead(200, {'Content-Type': 'text/html'});
  }
  else if (urlParts.pathname.lastIndexOf(".js") ==
    urlParts.pathname.length - 3)
  {
    res.writeHead(200, {'Content-Type': 'application/json'});
  }
  else
  {
    res.writeHead(200, {'Content-Type': 'text/plain'});
  }
```

Next, we read the content from the public directory below the Node.js server source and return it to the client:

```
  var c = fs.readFileSync('./public' + urlParts.pathname);
  res.end(c);
  return;
}
```

Finally, this big function gets registered as a listening HTTP server on port `1337` of the localhost, and we log that the server's started:

```
}).listen(1337, 'localhost');
console.log('Server running at http://localhost:1337');
```

 A real server probably shouldn't guess the MIME type of the returned data by looking at the incoming URL, but actually sniff the outgoing data and make a determination as to the MIME type and use that. There's a Node.js module magic that does just this; if you're a little less paranoid, you could use the file name suffix on the disk and hope that the content provider was correctly naming files.

That's it for the server, which you'll find in the ZIP for the samples that accompany this book.

Adding a dependency to jQuery to your web page

jQuery is a popular client-side framework for AJAX applications that gives you browser-independent support to search and manipulate the **Document Object Model** (**DOM**) and **Cascading Style Sheets** (**CSS**), perform AJAX queries, as well as include several HTML controls you can style using CSS. You need to include the source for jQuery in your page, either by pointing to a released version on the jQuery Content Delivery Network (CDN), or by going to `http://www.jquery.com` and downloading a copy of the framework for you to serve with your own application.

How to do it...

You'll need to include the jQuery library in your web page by starting a new json-example.html file, like this:

```
<!doctype HTML>
<html>
<head>
  <script type="text/javascript"
    src="/code.jquery.com/jquery-1.11.2.min.js"></script>
</head>
```

How it works...

These two lines include two scripts containing the minified version of the jQuery client library from the jquery.com CDN. This is probably what you want to do for production applications; the minified jQuery implementation is smaller than the full-blown library, so it's faster for your clients to download, and using the version on the CDN provides performance that may well be faster than what you can provide, unless you're hosting multiple servers at a major cloud provider such as Amazon Web Services or Microsoft Azure.

There's more...

If you don't want to include the minified versions—often the case when you're deep in your development cycle and want to debug your code—you can include the standard version served from your server. Just download the necessary files from `http://www.jquery.com/` and serve them from your server.

jQuery comes in two revisions: revision 1.x, which has support for older browsers, including Microsoft Internet Explorer 6 and above, and revision 2.x, which requires at least Microsoft Internet Explorer 9. Our examples will use jQuery 1.x, but never fear; the APIs we discuss are the same for jQuery 2.x.

See also

Head over to `http://www.jquery.com` to download jQuery or learn more about it. If you're looking for a JavaScript framework, it's probably worth looking at the jQuery learning center at `http://learn.jquery.com/`, or perhaps take a look at Packt Publishing's book, *Learning jQuery – Fourth Edition*, by *Jonathan Chaffer* and *Karl Swedberg*.

Requesting JSON content using jQuery

jQuery defines the variable `$`, which exposes methods for everything you want to do with the interface. (There are ways to rename that variable, say if you're working with another JavaScript environment that uses the same variable, but I don't recommend it). Among the methods `$` exposes is the `ajax` method, which you use to make AJAX queries. Let's see how.

How to do it...

Here's a whole page that makes an AJAX request. The AJAX code is in bold:

```
<!doctype HTML>
<html>
<head>
<script  type="text/javascript"
   src="//code.jquery.com/jquery-1.11.2.min.js"></script>
</head>
<body>

<p>Hello world</p>
<p>
   <div id="debug"></div>
</p>
<p>
   <div id="json"></div>
</p>
<p>
   <div id="result"></div>
</p>

<p>Powered by <a href="http://www.aprs.fi">aprs.fi</a></p>

<script>
$(function () {
   $('#debug').html("loaded... executing.");

   var request = {
     call: "kf6gpe-7"
   };

   $.ajax({
     type: "POST",
     url: "/",
     dataType:"json"  });
});

</script>
</body>
</html>
```

The HTML in this example is straightforward. It includes the jQuery modules, and then defines three `div` regions for the AJAX request to update when the request is complete. Let's look at the JavaScript function `doAjax` in more detail.

How it works...

The doAjax function, called when the page finishes loading, first sets the HTML contents of div named debug to the text "loaded... executing.". The $() syntax is the jQuery syntax to find an item in the DOM; you can find items by their ID by prefixing the name with a # (hash) symbol, such as a CSS selector. The value returned isn't the actual DOM element but a jQuery class that wraps the DOM element that exposes simple methods such as html to get or set the HTML contents of the item.

Next, we define the JSON object that has the particulars of our request, as we did in the previous chapter's recipes. It has one attribute, call, containing the call sign of the station we're interested in.

Next, we invoke the ajax method of $, passing a JavaScript object with the semantics of our request. It should have the following fields:

* The type field, which indicates the HTTP method of the request (such as POST or GET).

* The url field, which indicates the URL to which the request should be submitted.

* The data field, containing string data to be sent to the server for the request (if any). We'll see that used in the next recipe.

* The dataType field, indicating the type of data you're expecting from the server; an optional field, which can be xml, json, script, or html.

See also

Curious readers should consult the jQuery ajax method documentation available at http://api.jquery.com/jQuery.ajax/.

Sending JSON to your web server using jQuery

Sending JSON to your server using jQuery is easy. Just get the data in the JSON format and specify it using the ajax method argument's data field.

How to do it...

Let's look at `doAjax` again, this time modified to send our request JSON:

```
function doAjax() {
  $('#debug').html("loaded... executing.");

  var request = {
    call: "kf6gpe-7"
  };

  $.ajax({
    type: "POST",
    url: "/",
    data: JSON.stringify(request),
    dataType:"json"
  });
}

</script>
</body>
</html>
```

How it works...

The magic line in the previous listing is highlighted; it's the following line in the arguments passed to the `ajax` method:

```
    data: JSON.stringify(request),
```

Of course, we use `JSON.stringify` to encode the JavaScript object as JSON before assigning it to the data field.

Getting the progress of a request using jQuery

jQuery abstracts the various progress reporting mechanisms of the underlying `XMLHttpRequest` object in a platform-agnostic way, giving you the ability to determine whether your request succeeded or failed. You do this by registering functions that the jQuery AJAX handler will invoke when an error occurs or the results are successfully loaded.

How to do it...

Here's `doAjax` rewritten to support getting notifications on failure, regardless of whether the event succeeds or fails:

```
function doAjax() {
  $('#debug').html("loaded... executing.");

  var request = {
    call: "kf6gpe-7"
  };

  $.ajax({
    type: "POST",
    url: "/",
    data: JSON.stringify(request),
    dataType:"json",
  })
  .fail(function() {
    $('#debug').append("<br/>failed");
  })
  .always(function() {
    $('#debug').append("<br/>complete");
  });
}
```

The new methods here are the `fail` and `always` methods.

How it works...

jQuery uses a pattern called *chaining*, in which most of its methods return an instance of an object to which you can apply additional methods. So, methods such as `fail` and `always` operate on the same object, and return the same object, that encapsulates the return value from the `$.ajax` method call using chaining yields easier-to-read and easier-to-write code. In the case of `$.ajax`, what's returned is an instance of a jQuery `XMLHttpRequest` object, whose fields are a superset of the `XMLHttpRequest` object returned by the browser.

Here, I'm setting two event handlers on the return value to `$.ajax`: one for the failure case, in which the request fails for some reason, and one for the always case. Note that thanks to chaining, I could have reversed these and put the handler for the always case first and the handler for the failure case second. It's entirely up to you which you prefer.

The `always` and `failure` methods take a single function, which can take up to three arguments. In this case, I'm not using any of the available arguments and just appending some text to the HTML of the `div` region with the `id` debug. jQuery passes the `failure` event handler to the jQuery `XMLHttpRequest` object, a textual status message, and the error code associated with the failure, while it passes the `always` method to either those arguments on an error, or the data, a textual status message, and the jQuery `XMLHttpRequest` object.

There's more...

If you'd prefer, you can specify the fail event handler as a function in the attribute named error in the initial JavaScript object argument to `$.ajax`. Similarly, you can specify the always event handler as a function in the attribute named `complete` in the initial JavaScript object to `$.ajax`. While this puts all of the code in one place, I personally find that harder to read because the indentation can get unwieldy quickly.

Parsing the returned JSON using jQuery

Finally, it's time to see how to get the returned JSON from the server and use it. You'll do this by registering an event handler on `$.ajax` to receive the resulting JavaScript object, which jQuery helpfully deserializes from JSON for you.

How to do it...

To get the result from the AJAX request, we need to add an event handler to the jQuery
XMLHttpRequest object's done event, as follows:

```
function doAjax() {
  $('#debug').html("loaded... executing.");

  var request = {
    call: "kf6gpe-7"
  };

  $.ajax({
    type: "POST",
    url: "/",
    data: JSON.stringify(request),
    dataType:"json",
  })
  .fail(function() {
    $('#debug').html( $('#debug').html() + "<br/>failed");
  })
  .always(function() {
    $('#debug').html( $('#debug').html() + "<br/>complete");
  })
  .done(function(result) {
    $('#json').html(JSON.stringify(result));
    $('#result').html(result.call + ":" +
      result.lat + ", " + result.lng);
  });
}
```

How it works...

jQuery invokes the done event handler when the request successfully completes, passing
the resulting data as an argument. Because we specified a data type of json in the initial
call to $.ajax, jQuery helpfully uses JSON.parse to parse the return value, and passes the
JavaScript object we're interested in, saving us the need to call parse on our own.

Our `done` event handler does two things: it puts the JSON of the object (as serialized by the browser, not as returned by the server) in the `div` field with the ID `json`, and updates the result `div` with the station's call sign, latitude, and longitude from the resulting data. This gives us a web page that looks like this:

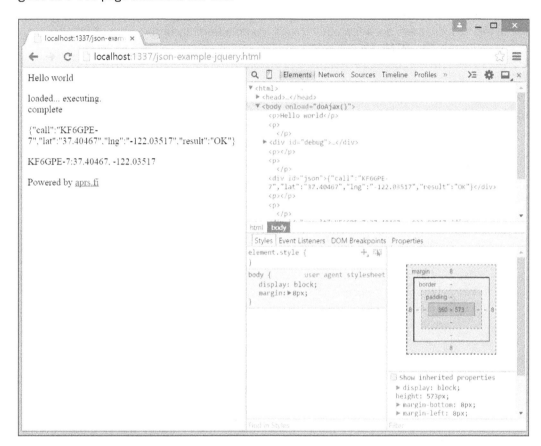

There's more...

If you prefer, you can register the event handler for successful completion by passing it as the `success` field of the initial request to `$.ajax`. Like `fail` and `always`, I prefer using chaining to set it explicitly because I think it's more readable.

Adding a dependency to AngularJS to your web page

Just as another JavaScript framework, you need to include AngularJS in your HTML. As you'll see in this section, there are a few other things you do differently to get set up. First, be sure that you create a new HTML file, such as `json-example-angular.html`.

How to do it...

Here's the HTML for our application in its entirety:

```
<!doctype HTML>
<html>
  <head>
  </head>

<body ng-app="aprsapp">
  <div ng-controller="AprsController">
    <button ng-click="doAjax()">Send AJAX Request</button>
    <div>{{debug}}</div>
    <div>{{json}}</div>
     <br/>
        <div>{{message}}<div>
  </div>

  <p>Powered by <a href="http://www.aprs.fi">aprs.fi</a></p>
<script type="text/javascript"
src="https://ajax.googleapis.com/ajax/libs/angularjs/1.3.2/angular.
min.js"></script>
<script src="json-example-angularjs.js"></script>
</body>
</html>
```

Let's look more closely at this HTML and see what's different.

How it works...

First, note that the `body` tag has the attribute `ng-app`, which is set to `aprsapp`. AngularJS applications are given defined names, and you reference those names in the JavaScript that implements the logic for your application.

Next, note that the `div` region containing our UI has the attribute `ng-controller`, which identifies the specific controller module responsible for handling the events for that part of the UI. We'll see how that's linked to the JavaScript in a moment. In that `div` are other `div` regions, whose contents are contained in double brackets, defining a document template that Angular.js fills out for you. This is a variable in AngularJS; at the time the controller loads, these variables in HTML will be replaced by the contents set by the controller. Each is a *model*, containing data to show.

Finally, we need to include the AngularJS module itself, as well as our JavaScript. It's customary to keep the JavaScript for your application in a separate file when working with AngularJS because this helps you enforce good separation between the appearance of the web application (contained in your HTML and CSS) and the implementation (contained in your JavaScript).

Now, let's look at the skeleton of the JavaScript for our page, which we put in the file `json-examnple-angular.js`:

```
var app = angular.module("aprsapp", []);

app.controller("AprsController", , ["$scope",
  function($scope) {
  $scope.json = "";
  $scope.message = "Loaded...";
}]);
```

This code defines a single AngularJS application, `aprsapp`. Note that this name has to match the name given to the `ng-app` attribute in your body tag. The code then registers a single controller for the application, `AprsController`. A controller is a function that takes at least one argument, the scope of the controller, which is where you define your data models and other variables. In our controller's scope, we set the initial values for two of our models: `json` and `message`.

See also

To get started with AngularJS, see its website at `https://angularjs.org` or the book *AngularJS Essentials* by *Rodrigo Branas* published by *Packt Publishing*.

Requesting JSON content using AngularJS

Angular defines a core object, $http, which you use to make HTTP requests of remote servers. It's passed to your controller when you initialize it.

How to do it...

Let's extend our controller to add a reference to the $http object and use it to make a request:

```
var app = angular.module("aprsapp", []);

app.controller("AprsController", ["$scope", "$http",
function($scope, $http) {
  $scope.json = "";
  $scope.message = "Loaded...";
  $scope.doAjax = function()
  {
    $scope.debug = "Fetching...";
    $scope.json= "";
    $scope.message = "";

    var promise = $http({
      url: "/",
      method: "POST",
    });
  };
}]);
```

Here, we define a function doAjax in our scope that will perform the asynchronous HTTP request. It updates our models so that the debug model contains a status message, and the json and message models are empty strings. Let's look at the $http object in more detail.

How it works...

Looking at the controller definition function, you can see that we passed not just the scope for the controller, but the $http object as well. It defines a function that takes one argument, a JavaScript object that defines the parameters of the HTTP request to make. In our example, we ask to make a POST request to the root of our server by setting the method field to POST and the url field to /.

The argument to the $http method can include these attributes:

▶ The method attribute, which indicates the HTTP method to use.

▶ The url attribute, which indicates the URL the method should be sent to.

▶ The params attribute, which is a map of strings or objects to send to the server; if the value is not a string, it will be encoded as JSON (more about that in the next recipe); the params attribute is appended to the URL.

▶ The data attribute, which is the data to be sent to the remote server.

▶ The headers attribute, which is a map of headers and header values to send to the remote server.

▶ The timeout attribute, which indicates how long to wait for a response.

The $http() method returns a *promise*, an object on which you will invoke other methods to register event handlers to detect errors and process data when it's been successfully sent. (We'll discuss the promise further in the recipes *Getting the progress of a request using AngularJS* and *Parsing the returned JSON using AngularJS*.)

There's more...

The $http object also defines separate methods get, post, put, delete, and patch, which make the appropriate HTTP requests. You can use them instead of the $http() method if you want to, omitting the method attribute. Like $http(), they all return a promise.

See also

For documentation on the $http() method and AngularJS support for AJAX, see https://docs.angularjs.org/api/ng/service/$http.

Sending JSON to your web server using AngularJS

Sending JSON with AngularJS is as easy as providing a data attribute in the argument to your $http() method call. AngularJS will even encode the object as JSON on your behalf.

How to do it...

Like before, we'll make an AJAX request. This time, we include a data attribute:

```
var app = angular.module("aprsapp", []);

app.controller("AprsController", ["$scope", "$http",
function($scope, $http) {
  $scope.json = "";
  $scope.message = "Loaded...";
  $scope.doAjax = function()
  {
    $scope.debug = "Fetching...";
    $scope.json= "";
    $scope.message = "";
    var request = {
      call: "kf6gpe-7"
    };
    var promise = $http({
      url: "/",
      method: "POST",
      data: request
    });
  };
}]);
```

How it works...

We define the JavaScript object request as we have in past examples, with a single call attribute containing the call sign of the station we're interested in. By passing this value as the data attribute in our argument to $http(), AngularJS converts the object to JSON and sends it to the server.

There's more...

If you use a method, such as $http.post(), pass the data as the second argument, like this:

```
$http.post("/", request);
```

You can also pass an optional configuration argument as the third argument. Such a configuration object will contain the attributes I described in the previous recipe for the request object.

Getting the progress of a request using AngularJS

The `$http()` method returns a promise, which is your way of determining what's happening with the request. It defines methods to which you can pass JavaScript functions that operate as event handlers when the underlying network transaction changes state.

How to do it...

The returned promise defines `success` and `error` methods, which take event handlers. To use them, we write the following code:

```
var app = angular.module("aprsapp", []);

app.controller("AprsController", ["$scope", "$http",
function($scope, $http) {
  $scope.json = "";
  $scope.message = "Loaded...";
  $scope.doAjax = function()
  {
    $scope.debug = "Fetching...";
    $scope.json= "";
    $scope.message = "";
    var request = {
      call: "kf6gpe-7"
    };
    var promise = $http({
      url:"/",
      method: "POST",
      data: request
    });
    promise.success(function(result, status, headers, config) {
      // handle success here
    });
    promise.error(function(data, status, headers, config) {
      alert("AJAX failed!");
    });
}]);
```

How it works...

On success, AngularJS invokes the function you register with the promise using the `success` method, passing it the result data, HTTP status, HTTP headers, and the configuration associated with the request. Here's where you'll deal with the results of your network transaction, which we discuss more in the next recipe. On any kind of failure, AngularJS invokes the callback you register with `error`, passing it the same data.

Note that `success` and `error` return the promise again, so you can chain these requests if you like.

Parsing the returned JSON using AngularJS

Handling the returned data with AngularJS is easy because it parses the returned JSON for you and passes the resulting object to the event handler you registered with the promise's `success` method.

How to do it...

Here's the complete client-side code for our AngularJS application. The `success` promise's callback just updates the models with the fields of the object we get as a result:

```
var app = angular.module("aprsapp", []);

app.controller("AprsController", function($scope, $http) {
  $scope.json = "";
  $scope.message = "Loaded...";
  $scope.doAjax = function()
  {
    $scope.debug = "Fetching...";
    $scope.json= "";
    $scope.message = "";
    var request = {
      call: "kf6gpe-7"
    };

    var promise = $http({
      url:"/",
      method: "POST",
      data: request
    });
    promise.success(function(result, status, headers, config) {
      $scope.debug = "Loaded.";
```

```
            $scope.json = result;
            $scope.message = result.call + ":" + result.lat + ", " +
               result.lng;
         });
         promise.error(function(data, status, headers) {
            alert("AJAX failed!");
         });
   }]);
```

How it works...

Because AngularJS handles the parsing of JSON, we can dereference the values in the resulting JSON directly when we populate the text in the message model. Note as well that we can assign the JSON model the result object, and when this is displayed, it'll show the JSON for the result object itself.

If you load up the HTML and JavaScript in Chrome and press the button that invokes doAjax, you should see something like this:

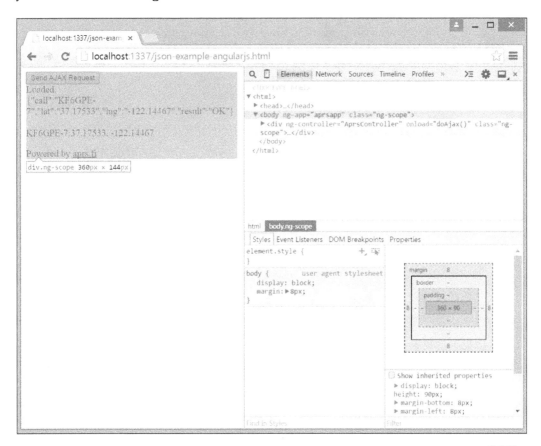

5
Using JSON with MongoDB

In this chapter, we will cover the following recipes:

- ▶ Setting up MongoDB
- ▶ Installing the MongoDB database driver for Node.js
- ▶ Installing the express module for Node.js
- ▶ Connecting to a MongoDB database using Node.js
- ▶ Creating a document in MongoDB using Node.js
- ▶ Searching for a document in MongoDB with Node.js
- ▶ Updating a document in MongoDB with Node.js
- ▶ Deleting a document in MongoDB using Node.js
- ▶ Using REST to search MongoDB
- ▶ Using REST to create a document in MongoDB
- ▶ Using REST to update a document in MongoDB
- ▶ Using REST to delete a document in MongoDB

Introduction

In this chapter, we look at how you can use MongoDB as the backend storage for your web application. While not completely focused on JSON, as you'll see, this chapter's recipes give you a leg up in managing document creation, reading, updating, and deleting with MongoDB, first directly in Node.js, and then, using a REST server built for Node.js and MongoDB so that you can manage documents from a network client, such as a web application.

Setting up MongoDB

Installing MongoDB varies by platform; on Linux, you may be able to use a package installer such as apt, while on Windows and Mac OS X (as well as on Linux, if you have a distribution that doesn't have a package manager with the MongoDB package), there are web downloads.

How to do it...

1. On Mac OS X and Windows, it's as easy as going to `http://www.mongodb.org/` and follow the download link. At the time of writing, MongoDB is at version 2.6.7; there's a release candidate for version 3.0, which we won't discuss further here.

   Mongo also provides packages for several common Linux distributions, including Debian and Fedora. There's also a package available for FreeBSD.

2. Once you download and install Mongo, you need to make a place for MongoDB to store its database.

   This varies by platform; on Windows, it's `c:\data\db`.

3. Once you do this, you can start the database server by running `mongod`. You may also want to add the path to the MongoDB client and server binaries in your path so that you can access them easily from the command line.

4. When you run MongoDB's server, you should see a bunch of log messages that read something like this:

```
C:\Program Files\MongoDB 2.6 Standard\bin\mongod.exe
--help for help and startup options
2015-02-15T13:10:07.909-0800 [initandlisten] MongoDB
starting : pid=13436 port=27017 dbpath=\data\db\
64-bit host=KF6GPE-SURFACE
2015-02-15T13:10:07.911-0800 [initandlisten]
targetMinOS: Windows 7/Windows Server 2008 R2
2015-02-15T13:10:07.913-0800 [initandlisten]
db version v2.6.7
2015-02-15T13:10:07.914-0800 [initandlisten] git
version: a7d57ad27c382de82e9cb93bf983a80fd9ac9899
2015-02-15T13:10:07.915-0800 [initandlisten]
 build info: windows sys.getwindowsversion
(major=6, minor=1, build=7601, pla
tform=2, service_pack='Service Pack 1')
BOOST_LIB_VERSION=1_49
2015-02-15T13:10:07.917-0800 [initandlisten]
allocator: system
2015-02-15T13:10:07.920-0800 [initandlisten] options: {}
2015-02-15T13:10:07.930-0800 [initandlisten] journal
dir=\data\db\journal
```

```
2015-02-15T13:10:07.931-0800 [initandlisten] recover
: no journal files present, no recovery needed
2015-02-15T13:10:07.967-0800 [initandlisten]
waiting for connections on port 27017
```

You'll want to note the hostname (in this example, `KF6GPE-SURFACE`) on which the server is running, and the port number, which by default should be `27017`.

5. To connect to the MongoDB server directly, you can run `mongo` on the command line, like this:

```
C:\>mongo
MongoDB shell version: 2.6.7
connecting to: test
>
```

6. To exit the `mongo` binary, hit *Ctrl + C* or type `exit`.

How it works...

The double-clickable installer and Linux packages install the mongod binary, which is the database, as well as the Mongo command-line client.

Installing the MongoDB database driver for Node.js

You'll need to install database drivers for Node.js, so that Node.js can talk directly to the MongoDB server.

How to do it...

To get the database drivers, simply go to the project directory where you've got your Node.js files and run the following command:

```
npm install mongodb
```

This command will download the database drivers and install them for Node.js.

Installing the express module for Node.js

The express module for Node.js makes it easy to build Representational State Transfer (REST) server applications using Node.js. REST is a powerful paradigm in web programming that uses the HTTP methods `GET`, `POST`, `PUT`, and `DELETE` to manage the create, read, update, and delete (often abbreviated as CRUD) actions for document management in web services.

Using REST, the URLs are nouns representing what you want to manipulate, and the HTTP methods are verbs that perform the actions on those nouns.

In the recipes that follow, we'll use node's express module to build a RESTful server that returns documents from Mongo, as well as supports the basic CRUD operations. Before you begin, you need to install three more modules.

How to do it...

You'll use npm, the Node.js package manager, to install the cross-object resource module to support cross-domain scripting, express module, and the body-parser module used by express. To do this, run in your project directory the following commands:

npm install cors

npm install express

npm install body-parser

You also need a basic application, or skeleton, for your REST server, which consists of routes between URLs on the REST server, the HTTP methods, and the functions that perform the necessary database operations. This skeleton consists of two Node.js scripts that use the express module and an HTML document.

The first Node.js script is the REST server itself, in `rest-server.js`, and it looks like this:

```
var express = require('express'),
  documents = require('./routes/documents'),
  cors = require('cors'),
  bodyParser = require('body-parser');

var app = express();

app.use(cors());
var jsonParser = bodyParser.json();

app.get('/documents', documents.findAll);
app.get('/documents/:id', documents.findById);
app.post('/documents', jsonParser, documents.addDocuments);
app.put('/documents/:id', jsonParser, documents.updateDocuments);
app.delete('/documents/:id', jsonParser,
documents.deleteDocuments);

app.listen(3000);
console.log('Listening on port 3000...');
```

How it works...

The package manager installs each of the modules, building them from source if needed. You'll need all three modules: the CORS module to support cross-domain scripting requests, the express module for the REST server framework, and finally, the body-parser module to translate client object bodies from JSON to JavaScript objects.

The skeleton script includes the express module, our *routes* file, which will define functions to handle each of the REST use cases, the CORS module, and the body-parser module needed by express to interpret object bodies sent by the client.

Once these are included, it defines an express module instance, named `app`, and configures it with CORS. This is necessary because by default, browsers won't make AJAX requests of servers at different domains than where their page content has come from, in order to prevent cross-side scripting attacks where servers are compromised and injected with malicious JavaScript. The CORS module sets up the necessary headers for the server to permit us to use our old Node.js server from the previous chapter on port `1337` to serve our content, and have our content access this REST server running on a different port.

Next, we get a reference to body-parser's JSON parser, which we'll use to parse the object bodies sent by the client for the insert and update requests. After this, we configure the Express app server instance with handlers for the top-level documents URL, which is used to access our MongoDB documents via REST. There are five possible operations at this URL:

- An HTTP GET of the URL `/documents` simply returns a list of all the documents in the database
- An HTTP GET of the URL `/documents/<id>` returns the document with the given ID in the database
- An HTTP POST to `/documents` with a document in the JSON format saves that document to the database
- An HTTP PUT to `/documents/<id>` with a document in the JSON format updates the document with the given ID to have the contents that the client passes
- An HTTP DELETE to `/documents/<id>` deletes the document with the given ID

Finally, the script starts the server listening on port `3000`, and logs the fact that the server has started.

Of course, we need to define the functions in the documents object; we do this in the file `routes/documents.js`, which to begin with should look like this:

```
var mongo = require('mongodb');

var mongoServer = mongo.Server,
    database = mongo.Db,
    objectId = require('mongodb').ObjectID;
```

```
var server = new mongoServer('localhost', 27017,
{auto_reconnect: true});
var db = new database('test', server);

db.open(function(err, db) {
  if(!err) {
    console.log("Connected to 'test' database");
    db.collection('documents',
    {strict:true},
    function(err, collection) {
      if (err) {
        console.log("Inserting sample data...");
        populate();
      }
    });
  }
});

exports.findById = function(req, res) {
  res.send('');
};

exports.findAll = function(req, res) {
  res.send('');
};

exports.addDocuments = function(req, res) {
  res.send('');
};

exports.updateDocuments = function(req, res) {
  res.send('');
};

exports.deleteDocuments = function(req, res) {
  res.send('');
};

var populate = function() {
var documents = [
  {
    call: 'kf6gpe',
    lat: 37,
```

```
    lng: -122   }
  ];
  db.collection('documents', function(err, collection) {
    collection.insert(wines, {safe:true},
    function(err, result) {});
    });
  };
```

The preceding code begins by importing the native MongoDB driver, setting variables to hold the server instance, database instance, and a converter interface that converts strings to MongoDB object IDs. Next, it creates an instance of the server connecting to our server instance (which must be running in order to succeed), and gets a reference to our database. Finally, it opens a connection to the database and inserts some sample data into the database if it's empty. (This code will be clearer after the first two recipes in this chapter, so if it seems a little confusing right now, just read along and you'll do fine!)

The remainder of the `routes/documents.js` file defines functions to handle each of the REST use cases we wired up in the `rest-server.js` script. We'll flesh out each of the functions as we go along in our recipes.

Finally, we need an HTML document that will access the REST server. Our document looks like this:

```html
<!DOCTYPE html>
<html>
<head>
<script type="text/javascript"
  src="http:////code.jquery.com/jquery-1.11.2.min.js"></script>
</head>
<body>

<p>Hello world</p>
<p>
<div id="debug"></div>
</p>
<p>
<div id="json"></div>
</p>
<p>
<div id="result"></div>
</p>

<button type="button" id="get" onclick="doGet()">Get</button><br/>
<form>
  Id: <input type="text" id="id"/>
  Call: <input type="text" id="call"/>
```

```
    Lat: <input type="text" id="lat"/>
    Lng: <input type="text" id="lng"/>
  <button type="button" id="insert"
      onClick="doUpsert('insert')">Insert</button>
  <button type="button" id="update"
  onClick="doUpsert('update')">Update</button>
  <button type="button" id="remove"
  onClick="doRemove()">Remove</button>
  </form>
  </body>
  </html>
```

We use a bit of jQuery to make the field access easier in the scripts (you'll see the scripts in the upcoming recipes for REST insertion, updating, removal, and querying). The HTML itself consists of three `div`, tags, one each for debugging, showing the raw JSON, and the result of each REST operation, and a form that lets you enter the fields you need to create, update, or delete records.

See also

For more information about the excellent Node.js express module, see `http://expressjs.com/`.

MongoDB is a powerful document database, and there's far more than we can cover here. For more information, check the Web, or look at the following resources from the PacktPub website:

▶ *Instant MongoDB* by *Amol Nayak*.

▶ *MongoDB Cookbook* by *Amol Nayak*.

Connecting to a MongoDB database using Node.js

Before your Node.js application can do anything with a MongoDB instance, it must connect to it over the network.

How to do it...

The Node.js drivers for MongoDB contain all of the necessary network code to establish and break connections with MongoDB running on your local or remote machine.

You need to include a reference to the native driver in your code and specify the URL of the database to connect to.

Here's a simple example that connects to the database and promptly disconnects:

```
var mongo = require('mongodb').MongoClient;

var url = 'mongodb://localhost:27017/test';

mongo.connect(url, function(error, db) {
  console.log("mongo.connect returned " + error);
  db.close();
});
```

Let's break this down line by line.

How it works...

The first line includes the native driver implementation for Mongo in your Node.js application, and extracts a reference to the `MongoClient` object it defines. This object contains the basic interface you need to interact with the database over the network, defining the `connect` and `close` methods.

The next line defines a string, `url`, that contains the URL of the database to connect to. The format of this URL is simple: it begins with the `mongodb` scheme to indicate that it's a URL for the MongoDB server. Next is the hostname and port (in this case, we connect to the localhost on mongo's default port, `27017`). Finally, we come to the name of the database to which you want to connect: in our case, `test`.

If you're using MongoDB's user access control to control access to your database, you'll need to specify a username and password, too. You do this just as you would for any other URL, like this:

```
mongodb://user:password@host:port/database
```

Whether to secure your database or not, of course, depends on your network topology and deployment; it's probably a good idea to do so in general.

We pass this URL to the mongo object's `connect` method, along with a function that the MongoDB native driver will call back once a connection has been successfully established, or if the connection failed. The driver invokes the callback function with two arguments: the first is an error code in the case of an error (or `null` on success), and a reference to a database object encapsulating the connection to the database you specified (which may be `null` if an error occurred establishing the connection).

Our callback function is very straightforward; it prints a message containing the value of the error code passed and then we disconnect from the database using `close`.

Always call `close` on your database object when you're done using it to ensure that the native driver can successfully clean up after itself and disconnect from the database. If you don't, you run leaking connections to the database.

See also

For more information about the native MongoDB driver for Node.js, see `http://docs.mongodb.org/ecosystem/drivers/node-js/`.

Creating a document in MongoDB using Node.js

The MongoDB database organizes its documents in *collections*, which are typically groups of documents that are related in some way (such as representing the same kinds of information). Because of this, your primary interface to documents is through a collection. Let's see how to get a collection and add a document to it.

A collection is a little like a table in relational databases, but there's no imposition that all documents in a collection have the same fields or the same types for each field. Think of it as an abstraction you can use to group similar kinds of documents.

How to do it...

Here's a function that inserts two static items into the collection named `documents` in our test database, which we put in its own file and run using Node.js:

```
var mongo = require('mongodb').MongoClient;

var url = 'mongodb://localhost:27017/test';

var insert = function(collection, callback) {
  var documents =
    [{
        call: 'kf6gpe-7', lat: 37.0, lng: -122.0
      },
      {
        call: 'kf6gpe-9', lat: 38.0, lng: -123.0
      }];
    // Insert some documents
```

```
      collection.insert(documents,
        function(error, result) {
          console.log('Inserted ' +result.length + ' documents ' +
            'with result: ');
          console.log(result);
          callback(result);
      });
    };

  mongo.connect(url, function(error, db) {
    console.log('mongo.connect returned ' + error);

    // Get the documents collection
    var collection = db.collection('documents');
    insert(collection, function(result) {
      db.close();
    });
  });
```

I've broken the code up into two pieces to make the callback structure clear: the insert function, which actually performs the insertions, and the connection callback, which calls the insertion function.

Let's take a closer look.

How it works...

The code begins in the same way, by getting a reference to the `MongoClient` object it uses to talk to the database. The connection code is essentially the same, too; the URL is the same, and the only change is the call to the database's `collection` method, passing the name of the collection we're interested in. The collection method returns a `collection` object, which offers methods for the CRUD operations we'll use on the collection of documents.

The `insert` function does a few things. It takes a collection on which you want to operate and a callback it will invoke when the insertion operation finishes or fails.

First, it defines a couple of static items to insert in the database. Note that these are plain old JavaScript objects; pretty much anything you can express as a JavaScript object, you can store in MongoDB. Next, it calls the collection's insert method, passing the objects to store and a callback the driver invokes after attempting the insertion.

The driver calls the callback again, passing an error value (which is `null` on success) and the JavaScript objects *as they were inserted* into the collection. Our callback function logs the results to the console, and calls back the insertion function's callback, which closes the database.

What does an inserted record look like? Here's an example from my console, once I ensure that we are running MongoDB as well:

```
PS C:\Users\rarischp\Documents\Node.js\mongodb> node .\example.js
mongo.connect returned null
Inserted 2 documents with result:
[ { call: 'kf6gpe-7',
    lat: 37,
    lng: -122,
    _id: 54e2a0d0d00e5d240f22e0c0 },
  { call: 'kf6gpe-9',
    lat: 38,
    lng: -123,
    _id: 54e2a0d0d00e5d240f22e0c1 } ]
```

Note that the objects have the same fields, but they also have an additional _id field, which is the unique id of the object in the database. In the next section, you will learn how to query on that.

There's more

What happens if you insert the same object multiple times into the database? Try it! You'll see that you get multiple copies of the object in the database; the fields aren't used to specify uniqueness (the exception is the _id field, which is unique across the database). Note that you can't specify an _id field yourself, unless you're assured that it's unique. To update an existing element, use the update method, which I described in the recipe *Updating a document in MongoDB with Node.js* in this chapter.

By default, MongoDB insertions operate quickly and might fail (say, if there's a transitory network problem, or if the server is temporarily overloaded). At the cost of performance, you can pass { safe: true } as the second argument to insert or to force the operation to wait for a successful operation or return an error if the operation fails.

See also

Refer to http://docs.mongodb.org/manual/reference/method/db.collection.insert/ for documentation about how to insert documents into MongoDB collections.

Searching for a document in MongoDB with Node.js

Being able to insert documents wouldn't do you much good if you didn't have a way to search for documents. MongoDB lets you specify a template on which to match, and returns objects matching that template.

As with insertions and updates, you'll work with a collection of documents, invoking the collection's `find` method.

How to do it...

Here's an example that finds all documents in the test collection with a call of `kf6gpe-7` and prints them to the console:

```
var mongo = require('mongodb').MongoClient;

var url = 'mongodb://localhost:27017/test';

mongo.connect(url, function(error, db) {
  console.log("mongo.connect returned " + error);

  var cursor = collection.find({call: 'kf6gpe-7'});
  cursor.toArray(function(error, documents) {
    console.log(documents);

    db.close();
  });
});
```

How it works...

After connecting to the database, we invoke `find` in the collection, which returns a cursor you can use to iterate through the found values. The `find` method takes a JavaScript object that acts as a template indicating the fields that you want to match; our example matches records with a slot named `call` equal to `kf6gpe-7`.

We don't iterate over the cursor but instead turn the entire collection of found values into a single array by using the cursor's `toArray` method. This is fine for our example because there aren't very many results, but be careful doing this with a database that has a lot of items! Fetching more than you really need from the database at once uses RAM and CPU resources better allocated to other parts of your application. It's better to iterate across the collection, or use paging, which we will discuss next.

There's more

The cursor has several methods you can use to iterate across your search results:

▶ The `hasNext` method returns `true` if the cursor has another item that can be returned

▶ The `next` method returns the next matching item from the cursor

▶ The `forEach` iterator takes a function and calls the function on each item of the cursor's results sequentially

When iterating over a cursor, it's best to use a while loop with `hasNext` and call next, or use `forEach`; don't just convert the results to an array and loop across the list! Doing so requires the database to fetch all of the records at once, which can be very memory-intensive.

At times, there may be still too many items to deal with; you can limit the number of returned items using the cursor methods `limit` and `skip`. The `limit` method limits the search to the number of items you pass as an argument; the `skip` method skips the number of items you specify.

In practice, the find method actually takes two arguments: a JavaScript object that is the criteria of the request and an optional JavaScript object defining the projection of the result set to new JavaScript objects.

The criteria can be an exact match criteria, as you've seen in the previous example. You can also perform matching using the special operations `$gt` and `$lt`, which let you filter the given fields by cardinal order as well. For example, you might write:

```
var cursor = collection.find({lng: { $gt: 122 } });
```

This will return all records with a `lng` field with a scalar value greater than 122.

The projection is a list of fields that you're interested in receiving from the database, each set to `true` or `1`. For example, the following code returns JavaScript objects containing only the `call` and `_id` fields:

```
var cursor = collection.find(
{call: 'kf6gpe-7'},
{call: 1, _id: 1});
```

See also

See `http://docs.mongodb.org/manual/reference/method/db.collection.find/` for documentation on the MongoDB find method, which the native driver makes available to your Node.js application.

Updating a document in MongoDB with Node.js

Updating a document in a collection is easy; simply use the collection's `update` method and pass the data you want to update.

How to do it...

Here's a simple example:

```
var mongo = require('mongodb').MongoClient;

var url = 'mongodb://localhost:27017/test';

var update = function(collection, callback) {
  collection.update({ call:'kf6gpe-7' },
    { $set: { lat: 39.0, lng: -121.0, another: true } },
    function(error, result) {
      console.log('Updated with error ' + error);
      console.log(result);
      callback(result);
    });
};

mongo.connect(url, function(error, db) {
  console.log("mongo.connect returned " + error);

  // Get the documents collection
  var collection = db.collection('documents');
  update(collection, function(result) {
    db.close();
  });
});
```

The pattern of this is identical to the `insert` method; `update` is an asynchronous method that invokes a callback with an error code and a result.

How it works...

The `update` method takes a template to match a document on and updates the first matching document with the field values you pass in the `$set` frame of the replacing JavaScript object. Note that you can add new fields to the document, too, as we did here; we add a new field `another` with a value of `true`.

You can specify a precise match to a specific document by passing an ID of the document in the `_id` field of the template you pass to update. The template you pass to `update` is a standard search query template, just like you'd pass to `find`.

There's more...

By default, `update` updates the first matching document. If you want it to update all the documents matching your template, pass the JavaScript object `{ multi: true }` as the (optional) third argument to update. You can also have `update` perform an *upsert*, that is, an update on a match, and an insertion if the match doesn't succeed. To do this, pass the JavaScript object `{ upsert: true }` as the third argument to update. These can be combined to match more than one document and upsert; if none are found, pass.

```
{
    multi: true,
    upsert: true
}
```

Like insert, you can also pass `safe: true` in this option's argument to ensure that the update attempts to succeed before returning at the cost of performance.

The `update` method passes the number of updated documents as its result to your callback.

See also

See the MongoDB native driver documentation for update at `https://github.com/mongodb/node-mongodb-native` or the MongoDB update method documentation at `http://docs.mongodb.org/manual/reference/method/db.collection.update/`.

Deleting a document in MongoDB using Node.js

At some point, you may want to delete a document in a collection using Node.js.

How to do it...

You do this using the `remove` method, which removes matching documents from the collection you specify. Here's an example of how to call `remove`:

```
var remove = function(collection, callback) {
  collection.remove({ call: 'kf6gpe-7'},
    function(error, result)
    {
```

```
        console.log('remove returned ' + error);
        console.log(result);
        callback(result);
    });
};
```

How it works...

This code removes documents that have a call field with the value `kf6gpe-7`. As you may have guessed, the search criteria used for `remove` can be anything you'd pass to find. The `remove` method removes *all* documents matching your search criteria, so be careful! Calling `remove({})` removes all of the documents in the current collection.

The `remove` method returns a count of the number of items removed from the collection.

See also

For more information about MongoDB's remove method, see its documentation at `http://docs.mongodb.org/manual/reference/method/db.collection.remove/`.

Using REST to search MongoDB

By now, that you might be wondering where JSON comes into play when using MongoDB. When you access a MongoDB database instance using a RESTful interface such as mongo-rest, the documents are transferred to the client using JSON. Let's see how to get a list of documents from MongoDB.

How to do it...

Using REST with Node.js and MongoDB takes several steps.

1. Be sure you've set up the REST server as we discussed in the introduction. You'll need to have created the files `rest-server.js`, `routes/documents.js`, and `mongo-rest-example.html` with the UI for our RESTful application, and run both the REST server and the document server with Node.js.

2. Second, be sure that you're running MongoDB.

3. Next, to process the REST `GET` request, we need to define the function `exports.findAll` in `documents.js`, which should look like this:

```
exports.findAll = function(req, res) {
  db.collection('documents', function(err, collection) {
    collection.find().toArray(function(err, items) {
      res.send(items);
```

```
    });
  });
};
```

4. After this, we need the `doGet` script in the `mongo-rest-example.html` file, which makes an AJAX `GET` request to the REST server for the documents in the database. This code performs an AJAX `GET` request to the server's `/documents/` URL, placing the resulting JSON in the `div` with the `id` json, and constructs an HTML table with one row for each resulting document in the result, providing columns for each document's ID, call sign, latitude, and longitude:

```
function doGet() {
  $.ajax({
    type: "GET",
    url: "http://localhost:3000/documents/",
    dataType: 'json',
  })
.done(function(result) {
    $('#json').html(JSON.stringify(result));
    var resultHtml =
'<table><thead>' +
'<th><td><b>id</b></td><td><b>call</b></td></th>' +
'<tbody>';
    resultHtml += '<td><b>lat</b></td><td><b>lng</b></td></tr>';

      $.each(result), function(index, item)
      {
        resultHtml += '<tr>';
        resultHtml += '<td>' + item._id + '</td>';
        resultHtml += '<td>' + item.call + '</td>';
        resultHtml += '<td>' + item.lat + '</td>';
        resultHtml += '<td>' + item.lng + '</td>';
        resultHtml += "</tr>";
      };
    $resultHtml += '</tbody></table>';

    $('#result').html(resultHtml);
  })
}
```

How it works...

The `findAll` method is a straightforward query of the database, matching all documents in the database using `find` in our collection. You can extend it to take a query template as a URL argument and then pass that as a URL-encoded argument to the GET URL.

You can also add additional arguments, such as arguments to limit and skip, which you should consider doing if you're processing a lot of data. Note that the Express module knows that it needs to JSON encode the JavaScript object to JSON before sending it to the client.

The doGet JavaScript is even simpler; it's a pure AJAX call, followed by a loop to unwrap the resulting returned JSON array into objects and present each object as a row in a table.

There's more

A good REST interface also provides an interface to query a specific item by ID because typically you'll want to query the collection, find something interesting in it, and then maybe do something with that specific ID. We define the method findById to take an ID in the incoming URL, convert the ID to a MongoDB object id, and then perform a find on just that ID, like this:

```
exports.findById = function(req, res) {
  var id = new objectId(req.params.id);
  db.collection('documents', function(err, collection) {
    collection.findOne({'_id':id}, function(err, item) {
      res.send(item);
    });
  });
};
```

Using REST to create a document in MongoDB

In principle, using REST to create a document is simple: create the JavaScript object on the client, encode it as JSON, and POST it to the server. Let's see how this works in practice.

How to do it...

There are two pieces to this: the client piece and the server piece.

1. On the client side, we need some way to get the data for our new MongoDB document. In our example, it's the fields of the form on the HTML page, which we wrap up and POST to the server using the client-side (in the HTML) method doUpsert:

```
function doUpsert(which)
{
Var id = $('#id').val();
var value = {};
  value.call = $('#call').val();
```

```
          value.lat = $('#lat').val();
          value.lng = $('#lng').val();

          $('#debug').html(JSON.stringify(value));

      var reqType = which == 'insert' ? "POST" : 'PUT';
        var reqUrl = 'http://localhost:3000/documents/' +
      (which == 'insert' ? '' : id);

        $.ajax({
          type: reqType,
          url: reqUrl,
          dataType: 'json',
          headers: { 'Content-Type' : 'application/json' },
          data: JSON.stringify(value)
        })
      .done(function(result) {
          $('#json').html(JSON.stringify(result));
      var resultHtml = which == 'insert' ? 'Inserted' : "Updated";
          $('#result').html(resultHtml);
        });
      }
```

2. The server accepts the posted document, automatically converts it from JSON using the body-parser module, and performs an insertion in the database, in the file documents.js:

```
exports.addDocuments = function(req, res) {
  var documents = req.body;
  db.collection('documents', {safe:true},
function(err, collection) {
collection.insert(documents, function(err, result) {
 if (err) {
res.send({'error':'An error has occurred'});
} else {
 console.log('Success: ' + JSON.stringify(result[0]));
res.send(result[0]);
        }
    });
  });
};
```

How it works...

The client code is used by both the insert and update buttons in the UI, which is why it's a little more complicated than you might first think. However, the only difference between an insert and an update in REST is the URL and the HTTP method (POST versus PUT), so it makes sense to use one method for both.

The client code begins by fetching the field values from the form using jQuery, and then sets the type of the request to POST for an update. Next, it constructs the REST URL, which should just be the base document's URL because there's no ID for a new document. Finally, it uses POST to send the JSON of the document to the server. The server code is straightforward: take the object body passed as a part of the request and insert it into the documents collection of the database, returning the result of the insertion to the client (this is a good pattern to follow, in case the client was the id of the newly created document for anything).

On the server side, JSON decoding is handled automatically because we registered our handler for the POST request using the jsonParser instance from the body-parser module like this:

```
app.post('/documents', jsonParser, documents.addDocuments);
```

> If you forget to pass a JSON parser to the routes registration, the request body field won't even be defined! So if you're inserting null documents in your database using Express, be sure to check that.

Using REST to update a document in MongoDB

Updating is identical to insertion, except that it needs a document ID and the client signals an update request with a HTTP POST request, rather than a PUT request.

How to do it...

The client code is exactly the same as the previous recipe; only the server code changes because it needs to extract the ID from the URL and perform an update instead of an insert:

```
exports.updateDocuments = function(req, res) {
  var id = new objectId(req.params.id);
  var document = req.body;
  db.collection('documents', function(err, collection) {
    collection.update({'_id':id}, document, {safe:true},
      function(err, result) {
```

```
        if (err) {
          console.log('Error updating documents: ' + err);
          res.send({'error':'An error has occurred'});
        } else {
          console.log('' + result + ' document(s) updated');
          res.send(documents);
        }
      });
    });
  };
```

Let's look at that in more detail.

How it works...

Returning to the client implementation for a moment in the previous recipe, you see that for an update, we included the ID in the URL. The updateDocuments method gets the ID from the request parameters and converts it to a MongoDB object id object, and then calls update with the document that the client passes with the POST request.

Using REST to delete a document in MongoDB

Like updating, deletion takes an object id, which we pass in the URL to the HTTP DELETE request.

How to do it...

The doRemove method gets the object id from the id field in the form, and posts a DELETE message to the server at a URL consisting of the base URL plus the object id:

```
function doRemove()
{
  var id = $('#id').val();

  if(id == "")''
  {
    alert("Must provide an ID to delete!");
    return;
  }

  $.ajax({
    type: 'DELETE',
```

```
         url: "http://localhost:3000/documents/" + id   })
      .done(function(result) {
        $('#json').html(JSON.stringify(result));
        var resultHtml = "Deleted";
        $('#result').html(resultHtml);
      });
      }
```

The deletion message handler on the server extracts the ID from the URL and then performs a `remove` operation:

```
    exports.deleteDocuments = function(req, res) {
      var id = new objectId(req.params.id);
      db.collection('documents', function(err, collection) {
        collection.remove({'_id':id}, {safe:true},
        function(err, result) {
          if (err) {
            res.send({'error':'An error has occurred - ' + err});
          } else {
            console.log('' + result + ' document(s) deleted');
            res.send({ result: 'ok' });
          }
        });
      });
    };
```

How it works...

On the client side, the flow is similar to the update flow; we get the ID from the `id` form element, and if it's null, it pops up an error dialog instead of doing the AJAX post. We make an AJAX post using the HTTP `DELETE` method, passing the `id` as the document name in the URL to the server.

On the server side, we get the ID from the request parameters, convert it to a MongoDB native object ID, and then pass it to the collection's remove method to remove the document. We then return either success or an error to the client.

6
Using JSON with CouchDB

In the last chapter, we looked at using JSON with MongoDB, a popular NoSQL database. In this chapter, we continue in the same vein, showing you how to use JSON with CouchDB, another popular NoSQL database. Here, you'll find recipes about:

- ▶ Installing and setting up CouchDB and Cradle
- ▶ Connecting to a CouchDB document using Node.js and Cradle
- ▶ Creating a CouchDB database using Node.js and Cradle
- ▶ Creating a document in CouchDB using Node.js and Cradle
- ▶ Setting up a data view in CouchDB with Node.js and Cradle
- ▶ Searching for a document in CouchDB with Node.js and Cradle
- ▶ Updating a document in CouchDB with Node.js and Cradle
- ▶ Deleting a document in CouchDB using Node.js and Cradle
- ▶ Using REST to enumerate CouchDB records
- ▶ Using REST to search CouchDB
- ▶ Using REST to upsert a document in CouchDB
- ▶ Using REST to delete a document in CouchDB

Introduction

CouchDB is a highly available, scalable document database. Like MongoDB, it is a NoSQL database; instead of organizing your data in tables related by IDs, you can place documents in the database. Unlike MongoDB, CouchDB has the interesting feature of *views*.

Documents you place in the DB with specific map and reduce functions that iterate across the data to provide specific views of the data by indexes that you can provide. Views are cached, making it easy to construct high-performance queries that return subsets of data or computed data-like reports.

The primary way you interact with CouchDB is via REST; even the Cradle driver we discuss in this chapter uses REST under the hood for document creation, updation, and deletion. You can also use REST for queries, either through document ID, or by converting an indexed query into a view.

In this chapter, we examine how to integrate CouchDB with Node.js using the Cradle module and how to make REST queries of a CouchDB from the Web.

Installing and setting up CouchDB and Cradle

CouchDB comes as a click-and-run installer for major platforms.

How to do it...

To begin, you first need to install the server. To do this, go to `http://couchdb.apache.org/` and download the installer appropriate for your platform. Before installing Cradle, be sure to run the installer.

Next, on a command line, run the following command to install Cradle:

```
npm install cradle
```

Finally, you need to enable cross-resource requests on the CouchDB server, to permit those requests on the Web. To do this, edit the `/etc/couchdb/default.ini` file, and change the following line:

```
enable_cors = false
```

With the following line:

```
enable_cors = true
```

You also need to indicate which origin servers you'll accept CORS requests from; to enable cross-resource requests for all domains, add the following line to `/etc/couchdb/default.ini` in the section labeled `[cors]`:

```
origins = *
```

If you want to be more specific, you can provide a comma-separated list of origin domains from which your HTML content and scripts are loaded.

Finally, you must start (or restart) the CouchDB server. On Windows, assuming you didn't install it as a service, go to the `bin` directory where you installed it and run `couchdb.bat`; on Linux and Mac OS X, kill and restart the CouchDB server process.

How it works...

The Cradle module is a popular way to integrate CouchDB with Node.js, although if you prefer, you could just use Node.js's request module and make REST requests directly.

See also

For more information about CouchDB, see the Apache CouchDB wiki at `http://docs.couchdb.org/en/latest/contents.html`.

Connecting to a CouchDB database using Node.js and Cradle

Although CouchDB provides a RESTful interface, you don't strictly need to make a database connection before using CouchDB; the Cradle module uses the notion of a connection to manage its internal state and there's still a connection object you need to create.

How to do it...

Here's how to include the Cradle module in your Node.js application and initialize it, getting a handle to a particular database:

```
var cradle = require('cradle');
var db = new(cradle.Connection)().database('documents');
```

How it works...

This code first includes the Cradle module, and then creates a new Cradle `Connection` object, setting its database to the database `documents`. This initializes Cradle with the default CouchDB host (localhost) and port (5984). If you need to override the host or port, you can do so by passing the host and port as the first and second arguments to the `Connection` constructor, like this:

```
var connection = new(cradle.Connection)('http://example.com',
  1234);
```

Creating a CouchDB database using Node.js and Cradle

Before you can use a database in CouchDB, you must create it.

How to do it...

Once you've obtained a handle to the database that you want to use, you should check to see whether it exists, and create it if it doesn't:

```
db.exists(function (err, exists) {
if (err) {
  console.log('error', err);
} elseif (!exists) {
{
  db.create();
}
});
```

How it works...

The `exists` method checks to see whether a database exists, calling the callback you provide with an error if one occurred and a flag indicating whether or not the database exists. If the database doesn't exist, you create it using the `create` method.

This is a common pattern for Cradle because the RESTful interface is, by nature, asynchronous. You'll pass the arguments to the method you want to perform and a callback function that the method invokes when it's complete.

 A common mistake that beginners make is to assume that you can call one of these methods without the callback function and then do something immediately that depends on the previous result. It won't work because the original operation hasn't taken place yet. Consider an insert and update on the same record. The insert completes asynchronously; if you try to do the update synchronously, there will be nothing to update!

There's more...

If you want to destroy a database, you can do so using the `destroy` method, which also takes a callback function like create. This destroys all records in the database as you might imagine, so use it with caution!

Creating a document in CouchDB using Node.js and Cradle

The Cradle module provides the `save` method to save a new document to the database. You pass the document to save and a callback to invoke when the operation completes or fails.

How to do it...

Here's how to save a simple record using `save`:

```
var item =   {
  call: 'kf6gpe-7',
  lat: 37,
  lng: -122
};

db.save(item, function (error, result) {
  if (error) {
    console.log(error);
    // Handle error
  } else {
    var id = result.id;
    var rev = result.rev;
    }
  });
```

How it works...

The save method returns a JavaScript object to your callback with fields for the newly created document IDs and an internal revision number, along with a field titled ok, which should be true. As you'll see in the recipe titled *Updating a Record in CouchDB with Node.js*, you need both the revision of a document you store and the ID in order to update it; otherwise, you end up creating a new document or receiving a failure to save the record. An example result might look like this:

```
{ ok: true,
  id: '80b20994ecdd307b188b11e223001e64',
  rev: '1-60ba89d42cc4bbc1301164a6ae5c3935' }
```

Setting up a data view in CouchDB with Node.js and Cradle

You can query CouchDB for documents by their ID, but of course, most of the time, you'll want to issue more complex queries, such as matching a field in a record against a particular value. CouchDB lets you define *views* of your data that consist of an arbitrary key in a collection of objects and then the objects derived from the view. When you specify a view, you're specifying two JavaScript functions: a map function that maps keys to items in your collection, and then an optional reduce function that iterates over the keys and values to create a final collection. In this recipe, we'll use the map function of a view to create an index of records by a single field.

How to do it...

Here's how to add a simple view to the database using CouchDB:

```
db.save('_design/stations', {
  views: {
    byCall: {
      map: function(doc) {
        if (doc.call) {
          emit(doc.call, doc);
        }
      }
    }
  }
});
```

This defines a single view for our database, the `byCall` view that consists of a map of call signs to documents in the database.

How it works...

Views are a powerful way to refer to documents in your database because you can construct arbitrarily simple or complex documents based on each document in the database.

Our example creates a single view, `byCall`, stored under the `views` directory (which is where you should put views) consisting of the call field of each record, and then the record is repeated. CouchDB defines the `emit` function to let you create pairings of keys for your view and view values; here, we use the `call` field as the key for each value and the document itself as the value. You could just as easily define a smaller subset of fields in a JavaScript object, or compute something across your JavaScript fields and emit that instead. You can define more than one view, each a field in the `views` field with a separate `map` function.

CouchDB caches views and updates them on demand as the database changes, storing the view data as B-trees, so updating and querying views are very fast at run time. As you'll see in the next example, searching a view for a specific key is as simple as passing the key to the view.

Views are just documents in CouchDB, stored in a special location with functions instead of data values. Internally, CouchDB compiles the view's functions when it stores the view and runs them when there are changes such as insertions and deletions to the store.

See also

▶ For more information on the CouchDB view concept, see the CouchDB wiki at `http://wiki.apache.org/couchdb/Introduction_to_CouchDB_views`

▶ CouchDB view API documentation at `http://wiki.apache.org/couchdb/HTTP_view_API`.

Searching for a document in CouchDB with Node.js and Cradle

Searching for a document in CouchDB is a matter of querying a specific view for a specific key. The Cradle module defines the `view` function to do this.

How to do it...

You'll pass the URL of the view for the query you want to execute, and then pass the key for which you're searching as the key parameter, like this:

```
var call = "kf6gpe-7";
db.view('stations/byCall/key="' + call + '"',
  function (error, result) {
    if (result) {
      result.forEach(function (row) {
        console.log(row);
});
});
```

In addition to passing the view and key you're looking for, you must pass a callback function that handles the result.

How it works...

Here, we're searching the `byCall` view for a call sign of `kf6gpe-7`. Recall from the last recipe that the view consists of a map of call signs in the `call` field to records; when we issue the view request with the database's `view` method, it searches that map for records with keys matching `kf6gpe-7`, and returns a result that consists of an array of matching records. The method uses the array's `forEach` method to iterate across each item of the array, writing each item one at a time to the console.

There's more

You can pass a number of arguments to a view. The most obvious is the `key` argument, which lets you pass a single key to match. There's also the `keys` argument, which lets you pass an array of keys. You can also pass `startkey` and `endkey` instead, to query a view for a range of keys. If you need to limit the results, you can use the `limit` and `skip` arguments to limit the number of results, or skip the first *n* results that match.

If you know a document's ID, you can also use Cradle's `get` method to get the object directly:

```
db.get(id, function(error, doc) {
  console.log(doc);
});
```

See also

For details about the query operations you can invoke on views, see the CouchDB wiki at `http://wiki.apache.org/couchdb/HTTP_view_API#Querying_Options`.

Updating a document in CouchDB with Node.js and Cradle

The Cradle module defines the `merge` method to let you update an existing document.

How to do it...

Here's an example where we change the call of a record from `kf6gpe-7` to `kf6gpe-9` by specifying its ID, and then performing a merge with the new data:

```
var call = "kf6gpe-7";

db.merge(id, {call: 'kf6gpe-9'}, function(error, doc) {
  db.get(id, function(error, doc) {
```

```
      console.log(doc);
    });
  });
```

As you can see from the function, `merge` takes the ID of the record to merge, and a JavaScript object with the fields to replace or add to the existing object. You can also pass a callback, which is invoked by merge when the operation completes. The error value will be non-zero in the event of an error, and the document is returned as the second argument. Here, we just log the contents of the revised document to the console.

Deleting a document in CouchDB using Node.js and Cradle

To remove a record, you use the Cradle module's `remove` method and pass the ID of the document you want to remove.

How to do it...

Here's an example of remove:

```
db.remove(id);
```

Passing an ID removes the document with the given ID.

There's more...

If you have more than one document to remove, you could iterate across all documents, the way the following code does, removing each document in turn:

```
db.all(function(err, doc) {
  for(var i = 0; i < doc.length; i++) {
    db.remove(doc[i].id, doc[i].value.rev, function(err, doc) {
      console.log('Removing ' + doc._id);
    });
  }
});
```

This is a more complex use of `remove`; it takes the document's ID, the revision of the document, and a callback function, which logs to the console the ID of each document that was removed.

Using REST to enumerate CouchDB records

REST semantics dictate that to fetch the full contents of a collection of objects, we just send a GET request to the collection's root. We can do that from a web client to a CouchDB with CORS enabled using jQuery with a single call.

How to do it...

Here's some HTML, jQuery, and JavaScript that enumerate all items in a CouchDB view and shows some of the fields of each objects in an embedded table:

```
<!DOCTYPE html>
<html>
<head>
<script src="//code.jquery.com/jquery-1.11.2.min.js"></script>
<script src="//code.jquery.com/jquery-migrate-1.2.1.min.js"></script>
</head>
<body>

<p>Hello world</p>
<p>
  <div id="debug"></div>
</p>
<p>
  <div id="json"></div>
</p>
<p>
  <div id="result"></div>
</p>

<button type="button" id="get" onclick="doGet()">Get</button><br/>
<form>
  Id: <input type="text" id="id"/>
  Rev: <input type="text" id="rev"/>
  Call: <input type="text" id="call"/>
  Lat: <input type="text" id="lat"/>
  Lng: <input type="text" id="lng"/>
  <button type="button" id="insert"
    onClick="doUpsert('insert')">Insert</button>
  <button type="button" id="update"
    onClick="doUpsert('update')">Update</button>
  <button type="button" id="remove"
    onClick="doRemove()">Remove</button>
</form><br/>
```

```
<script>

function doGet() {
  $.ajax({
    type: "GET",
    url:
"http://localhost:5984/documents/_design/stations/_view/byCall",
    dataType:"json",
  })
  .done(function(result) {
    $('#json').html(JSON.stringify(result));
    var resultHtml = '<table><tr><td><b>id</b></td>';
    resultHtml += '<td><b>revision</b></td><td><b>call</b></td>';
    resultHtml += '<td><b>lat</b></td><td><b>lng</b></td></tr>';
    for(var i = 0; i < result.rows.length; i++)
    {
      var item = result.rows[i]
      resultHtml += "<tr>";
      resultHtml += "<td>" + item.id + "</td>";
      resultHtml += "<td>" + item.value._rev + "</td>";
      resultHtml += "<td>" + item.value.call + "</td>";
      resultHtml += "<td>" + item.value.lat + "</td>";
      resultHtml += "<td>" + item.value.lng + "</td>";
      resultHtml += "</tr>";
    }
    $('#result').html(resultHtml);
  });
}
</script>
</html>
```

How it works...

The HTML is straightforward; it includes jQuery, and then defines three `div` regions to show the results of the request. After that, it defines a form with fields for the document's ID, revision, callsign, latitude and longitude, and adds buttons to get a list of records, perform an insertion or update, and remove a record.

We need to have the `byCall` view defined for this to work (see the recipe *Setting up a Data View in CouchDB Using Node.js* for how to set up the data view using Node.js). This code performs a HTTP GET to the view's base URL, and takes the returned JavaScript object (parsed from the JSON by jQuery) and formats it as a table. (Note that we could have appended a specific key to the URL to obtain only a single URL).

The format of the REST response is a little different than if you query the collection using Cradle; you're seeing the actual response from CouchDB rather than the result massaged by Cradle. It looks something like this in the raw form:

```
{"total_rows":1,"offset":0,
  "rows":[
     {"id":"80b20994ecdd307b188b11e223001e64",
"key":"kf6gpe-7",
        "value":{
"_id":"80b20994ecdd307b188b11e223001e64",
"_rev":"1-60ba89d42cc4bbc1301164a6ae5c3935",
"call":"kf6gpe-7","lat":37,"lng":-122
        }
     }
  ]
}
```

Specifically, the `total_rows` field indicates how many rows are in the result in the collection; the `offset` field indicates how many rows were skipped in the collection before the first row returned, and then the `rows` array contains each key-value pair generated by the map of the view. The rows field has an ID field, the unique ID generating that map entry, the key emitted by the map operation, and the record emitted by the map operation.

Note that if you perform a `GET` request on the base URL for the database, you get something different; not all the records in the database, but information about the database:

```
{"db_name":"documents",
"doc_count":5,
"doc_del_count":33,
"update_seq":96,
"purge_seq":0,
"compact_running":false,
"disk_size":196712,
"data_size":6587,
"instance_start_time":"1425000784214001",
"disk_format_version":6,
"committed_update_seq":96
}
```

These fields may vary depending on the version of CouchDB that you're running.

See also

For information about the HTTP REST interface to CouchDB, see the documentation at `http://wiki.apache.org/couchdb/HTTP_Document_API`.

Using REST to search CouchDB

Using REST to search CouchDB uses a view with a map to create your index, which you insert once, and then a GET HTTP request.

How to do it...

We can modify the previous `doGet` function to search for a particular call sign, like this:

```
function doGet(call) {
  $.ajax({
    type: "GET",
    url:
"http://localhost:5984/documents/_design/stations/_view/byCall" +
      (call != null & call != '') ? ( '?key=' + call ) : '' ),
    dataType:"json",
  })
  .done(function(result) {
    $('#json').html(JSON.stringify(result));
    var resultHtml = '<table><tr><td><b>id</b></td>';
    resultHtml += '<td><b>revision</b></td><td><b>call</b></td>';
    resultHtml += '<td><b>lat</b></td><td><b>lng</b></td></tr>';
    for(var i = 0; i < result.rows.length; i++)
    {
      var item = result.rows[i]
      resultHtml += "<tr>";
      resultHtml += "<td>" + item.id + "</td>";
      resultHtml += "<td>" + item.value._rev + "</td>";
      resultHtml += "<td>" + item.value.call + "</td>";
      resultHtml += "<td>" + item.value.lat + "</td>";
      resultHtml += "<td>" + item.value.lng + "</td>";
      resultHtml += "</tr>";
    }
    $('#result').html(resultHtml);
  });
}
```

How it works...

The relevant lines are the argument call, passed to `doGet`, and the construction of the URL to which we dispatch the `GET` request. Note how we check for a null or empty call to fetch the entire collection; your code may want to do something different like report an error, especially if the collection is large.

Note that the view must exist prior to doing this. I like to use Node.js to create my views once when I initially update my database, and update the views if I make changes, rather than embedding the views in the client, because for most applications there are many clients and there's no point in thrashing the store with the same views being updated by many clients.

Using REST to upsert a document in CouchDB

There's no REST equivalent of Cradle's merge when you want to perform an upsert; instead, insertion is handled by a HTTP POST request, while updating is handled by a PUT request.

How to do it...

Here's some HTML and a doUpsert method that looks at form elements on your HTML page and either creates a new document in the database or updates an existing document if one already exists and you pass both the ID and revision fields:

```
<!DOCTYPE html>
<html>
<head>
<script src="//code.jquery.com/jquery-1.11.2.min.js"></script>
<script src="//code.jquery.com/jquery-migrate-1.2.1.min.js"></script>
</head>
<body>

<p>Hello world</p>
<p>
  <div id="debug"></div>
</p>
<p>
  <div id="json"></div>
</p>
<p>
  <div id="result"></div>
</p>

<button type="button" id="get" onclick="doGet()">Get</button><br/>
<form>
  Id: <input type="text" id="id"/>
  Rev: <input type="text" id="rev"/>
  Call: <input type="text" id="call"/>
  Lat: <input type="text" id="lat"/>
  Lng: <input type="text" id="lng"/>
```

```
    <button type="button" id="insert"
      onClick="doUpsert('insert')">Insert</button>
    <button type="button" id="update"
      onClick="doUpsert('update')">Update</button>
    <button type="button" id="remove"
      onClick="doRemove()">Remove</button>
</form><br/>

<script>

function doUpsert();
{
  var value = {};
  var which = null;
  id = $('#id').val();

  if (id != '') {
    which = 'insert';
  }

  value.call = $('#call').val();
  value.lat = $('#lat').val();
  value.lng = $('#lng').val();

  if (which != 'insert') {
    value._rev = $('#rev').val();
    value._id = id;
  }

  $('#debug').html(JSON.stringify(value));

  var reqType = which == 'insert' ? "POST" : "PUT";
  var reqUrl = "http://localhost:5984/documents/" +
    (which == 'insert' ? '' : id);

  $.ajax({
    type: reqType,
    url: reqUrl,
    dataType:"json",
    headers: { 'Content-Type' : 'application/json' },
    data: JSON.stringify(value)
  })
  .done(function(result) {
    $('#json').html(JSON.stringify(result));
```

```
          var resultHtml = which == 'insert' ? "Inserted" : "Updated";
          $('#result').html(resultHtml);
        })
   }
   </script>
</html>
```

How it works...

The doUpsert method begins by defining an empty JavaScript object, which is what we'll populate and send to the server with either a PUT or POST request. We then extract the values of the form fields; if the id field is set with an ID, we assume that this is an update, rather than an insert, and also capture the contents of the revision field named rev.

If there is no ID value set, it's an insert operation, and we set the request type to POST. If it's an update, we set the request type to PUT, indicating to CouchDB that this is an update.

Next, we construct the URL; the URL for a document update must include the ID of the document to be updated; that's how CouchDB knows which document to update.

Finally, we perform an AJAX request of the type we previously defined (either PUT or POST). Of course, we JSON-encode the JavaScript document we send to the server, and include a header indicating that the document being sent is JSON.

The returned value is a JSON document (converted by jQuery to a JavaScript object) that consists of the ID and revision of the inserted document, something like this:

```
{ "ok":true,
  "id":"80b20994ecdd307b188b11e223001e64",
  "rev":"2-e7b2a85adef5e721634bdf9a5707eb42"}
```

 Note that your request to update a document must include both the document's current revision and ID, or the PUT request will fail with a HTTP 409 error.

Using REST to delete a document in CouchDB

You denote a RESTful deletion of a document by sending a HTTP DELETE request with the ID and revision of the document to be deleted.

How to do it...

Using the HTML from the previous recipe, here's a script that extracts the ID and revision from the form fields, does some simple error checking, and sends a deletion request to the server for the document with the indicated ID and revision:

```
function doRemove()
{
  id = $('#id').val();
  rev = $('#rev').val();
  if (id == '')
  {
    alert("Must provide an ID to delete!");
    return;
  }
  if (rev == '')
  {
    alert("Must provide a document revision!");
    return;
  }


  $.ajax({
    type: "DELETE",
    url: "http://localhost:5984/documents/" + id + '?rev=' + rev,
  })
  .done(function(result) {
    $('#json').html(JSON.stringify(result));
    var resultHtml = "Deleted";
    $('#result').html(resultHtml);
  })
}
```

How it works...

The code begins by extracting the ID and revision from the form elements and popping up error dialogs if either is empty. Next, construct an AJAX HTTP DELETE request. The URL is the URL of the document—the database and document ID—with the revision of the document as an argument passed with the name `rev`. Assuming that you specify the ID and revision correctly, you'll get a response identical to that of an update: the ID and revision of the document that was removed. If it fails, you'll get an HTTP error.

7
Using JSON in a Type-safe Manner

In this chapter, we build on the recipes from *Chapter 1, Reading and Writing JSON on the Client*, showing you how you can use strong typing in your applications with JSON using C#, Java, and TypeScript. You'll find the following recipes:

- ▶ How to deserialize an object using Json.NET
- ▶ How to handle date and time objects using Json.NET
- ▶ How to deserialize an object using gson for Java
- ▶ How to use TypeScript with Node.js
- ▶ How to annotate simple types using TypeScript
- ▶ How to declare interfaces using TypeScript
- ▶ How to declare classes with interfaces using TypeScript
- ▶ Using json2ts to generate TypeScript interfaces from your JSON

Introduction

While some say that strong types are for weak minds, the truth is that strong typing in programming languages can help you avoid whole classes of errors in which you mistakenly assume that an object of one type is really of a different type. Languages such as C# and Java provide strong types for exactly this reason.

Fortunately, the JSON serializers for C# and Java support strong typing, which is especially handy once you've figured out your object representation and simply want to map JSON to instances of classes you've already defined. In *Chapter 1, Reading and Writing JSON on the Client*, you saw how to convert from a C# or Java class to JSON, as well as how to convert the JSON back to an untyped object; in this chapter, we use Json.NET for C# and gson for Java to convert from JSON to instances of classes you define in your application.

Finally, we take a look at TypeScript, an extension of JavaScript that provides compile-time checking of types, compiling to plain JavaScript for use with Node.js and browsers. We'll look at how to install the TypeScript compiler for Node.js, how to use TypeScript to annotate types and interfaces, and how to use a web page by Timmy Kokke to automatically generate TypeScript interfaces from JSON objects.

How to deserialize an object using Json.NET

In this recipe, we show you how to use Newtonsoft's Json.NET to deserialize JSON to an object that's an instance of a class. We'll use Json.NET, which we mentioned in *Chapter 1, Reading and Writing JSON on the Client*, because although this works with the existing .NET JSON serializer, there are other things that I want you to know about Json.NET, which we'll discuss in the next two recipes.

Getting ready

To begin, you need to be sure you have a reference to Json.NET in your project. The easiest way to do this is to use NuGet; launch NuGet, search for Json.NET, and click on **Install**, as shown in the following screenshot:

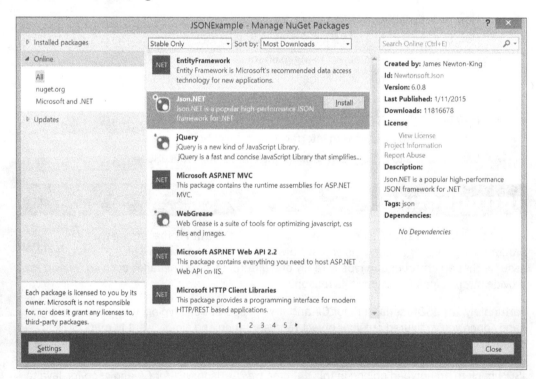

You'll also need a reference to the `Newonsoft.Json` namespace in any file that needs those classes with a `using` directive at the top of your file:

```
usingNewtonsoft.Json;
```

How to do it...

Here's an example that provides the implementation of a simple class, converts a JSON string to an instance of that class, and then converts the instance back into JSON:

```
using System;
usingNewtonsoft.Json;

namespaceJSONExample
{

  public class Record
  {
    public string call;
    public double lat;
    public double lng;
  }

  class Program
  {
    static void Main(string[] args)
      {
        String json = @"{ 'call': 'kf6gpe-9',
        'lat': 21.9749, 'lng': 159.3686 }";

        var result = JsonConvert.DeserializeObject<Record>(
          json, newJsonSerializerSettings
            {
        MissingMemberHandling = MissingMemberHandling.Error
          });
        Console.Write(JsonConvert.SerializeObject(result));

        return;
        }
    }
}
```

How it works...

In order to deserialize the JSON in a type-safe manner, we need to have a class that has the same fields as our JSON. The `Record` class, defined in the first few lines does this, defining fields for `call`, `lat`, and `lng`.

The `Newtonsoft.Json` namespace provides the `JsonConvert` class with static methods `SerializeObject` and `DeserializeObject`. `DeserializeObject` is a generic method, taking the type of the object that should be returned as a type argument, and as arguments the JSON to parse, and an optional argument indicating options for the JSON parsing. We pass the `MissingMemberHandling` property as a setting, indicating with the value of the enumeration `Error` that in the event that a field is missing, the parser should throw an exception. After parsing the class, we convert it again to JSON and write the resulting JSON to the console.

There's more...

If you skip passing the `MissingMember` option or pass `Ignore` (the default), you can have mismatches between field names in your JSON and your class, which probably isn't what you want for type-safe conversion. You can also pass the `NullValueHandling` field with a value of `Include` or `Ignore`. If `Include`, fields with null values are included; if `Ignore`, fields with Null values are ignored.

See also

The full documentation for Json.NET is at `http://www.newtonsoft.com/json/help/html/Introduction.htm`.

Type-safe deserialization is also possible with JSON support using the .NET serializer; the syntax is similar. For an example, see the documentation for the JavaScriptSerializer class at `https://msdn.microsoft.com/en-us/library/system.web.script.serialization.javascriptserializer(v=vs.110).aspx`.

How to handle date and time objects using Json.NET

Dates in JSON are problematic for people because JavaScript's dates are in milliseconds from the epoch, which are generally unreadable to people. Different JSON parsers handle this differently; Json.NET has a nice `IsoDateTimeConverter` that formats the date and time in ISO format, making it human-readable for debugging or parsing on platforms other than JavaScript. You can extend this method to converting any kind of formatted data in JSON attributes, too, by creating new converter objects and using the converter object to convert from one value type to another.

How to do it...

Simply include a new `IsoDateTimeConverter` object when you call `JsonConvert.Serialize`, like this:

```
string json = JsonConvert.SerializeObject(p,
newIsoDateTimeConverter());
```

How it works...

This causes the serializer to invoke the `IsoDateTimeConverter` instance with any instance of date and time objects, returning ISO strings like this in your JSON:

```
2015-07-29T08:00:00
```

There's more...

Note that this can be parsed by Json.NET, but not JavaScript; in JavaScript, you'll want to use a function like this:

```
Function isoDateReviver(value) {
  if (typeof value === 'string') {
  var a = /^(\d{4})-(\d{2})-(\d{2})T(\d{2}):(\d{2}):(\d{2}(?:\.\d*)?)
(?:([\+-])(\d{2})\:(\d{2}))?Z?$/
  .exec(value);
  if (a) {
     var utcMilliseconds = Date.UTC(+a[1],
           +a[2] - 1,
           +a[3],
           +a[4],
           +a[5],
           +a[6]);
        return new Date(utcMilliseconds);
    }
  }
return value;
}
```

The rather hairy regular expression on the third line matches dates in the ISO format, extracting each of the fields. If the regular expression finds a match, it extracts each of the date fields, which are then used by the `Date` class's UTC method to create a new date.

Note that the entire regular expression—everything between the/ characters—should be on one line with no whitespace. It's a little long for this page, however!

See also

For more information on how Json.NET handles dates and times, see the documentation and example at `http://www.newtonsoft.com/json/help/html/ SerializeDateFormatHandling.htm`.

How to deserialize an object using gson for Java

Like Json.NET, gson provides a way to specify the destination class to which you're deserializing a JSON object. In fact, it's the same method you used in the recipe *Reading and writing JSON in Java*, in *Chapter 1, Reading and Writing JSON on the Client*.

Getting ready

You'll need to include the gson JAR file in your application, just as you would for any other external API.

How to do it...

You use the same method as you use for type-unsafe JSON parsing using gson using `fromJson`, except you pass the class object to gson as the second argument, like this:

```
// Assuming we have a class Record that looks like this:
/*
class Record {
  private String call;
  private float lat;
  private float lng;
    // public API would access these fields
}
*/

Gson gson = new com.google.gson.Gson();
String json = "{ \"call\": \"kf6gpe-9\",
\"lat\": 21.9749, \"lng\": 159.3686 }";
Record result = gson.fromJson(json, Record.class);
```

How it works...

The `fromGson` method always takes a Java class; in *Chapter 1, Reading and Writing JSON on the Client*, the class we were deserializing to was `JsonElement`, which handles the general dynamic nature of JSON. In the example in this recipe, we convert directly to a plain old Java object that our application can use without needing to use the dereferencing and type conversion interface of `JsonElement` that gson provides.

There's more...

The gson library can also deal with nested types and arrays as well. You can also hide fields from being serialized or deserialized by declaring them `transient`, which makes sense because transient fields aren't serialized.

See also

The documentation for gson and its support for deserializing instances of classes is at `https://sites.google.com/site/gson/gson-user-guide#TOC-Object-Examples`.

How to use TypeScript with Node.js

Using TypeScript with Visual Studio is easy; it's just part of the installation of Visual Studio for any version after Visual Studio 2013 Update 2. Getting the TypeScript compiler for Node.js is almost as easy—it's an `npm install` away.

How to do it...

On a command line with npm in your path, run the following command:

```
npm install -g typescript
```

The npm option `-g` tells npm to install the TypeScript compiler globally, so it's available to every Node.js application you write. Once you run it, npm downloads and installs the TypeScript compiler binary for your platform.

There's more...

Once you run this command to install the compiler, you'll have the TypeScript compiler tsc available on the command line. Compiling a file with tsc is as easy as writing the source code and saving in a file that ends in .ts extension, and running tsc on it. For example, given the following TypeScript saved in the file hello.ts:

```
function greeter(person: string) {
  return "Hello, " + person;
}

var user: string = "Ray";

console.log(greeter(user));
```

Running tschello.ts at the command line creates the following JavaScript:

```
function greeter(person) {
  return "Hello, " + person;
}

var user = "Ray";

console.log(greeter(user));
```

Try it!

As we'll see in the next section, the function declaration for greeter contains a single TypeScript annotation; it declares the argument person to be string. Add the following line to the bottom of hello.ts:

```
console.log(greeter(2));
```

Now, run the tschello.ts command again; you'll get an error like this one:

```
C:\Users\rarischp\Documents\node.js\typescript\hello.ts(8,13):
error TS2082: Supplied parameters do not match any signature
of call target:
      Could not apply type 'string' to argument 1 which is
      of type 'number'.
C:\Users\rarischp\Documents\node.js\typescript\hello.ts(8,13):
error TS2087: Could not select overload for 'call' expression.
```

This error indicates that I'm attempting to call greeter with a value of the wrong type, passing a number where greeter expects a string. In the next recipe, we'll look at the kinds of type annotations TypeScript supports for simple types.

See also

The TypeScript home page, with tutorials and reference documentation, is at `http://www.typescriptlang.org/`.

How to annotate simple types using TypeScript

Type annotations with TypeScript are simple decorators appended to the variable or function after a colon. There's support for the same primitive types as in JavaScript, and to declare interfaces and classes, which we will discuss next.

How to do it...

Here's a simple example of some variable declarations and two function declarations:

```
function greeter(person: string): string {
  return "Hello, " + person;
}

function circumference(radius: number) : number {
  var pi: number = 3.141592654;
  return 2 * pi * radius;
}

var user: string = "Ray";

console.log(greeter(user));
console.log("You need " +
circumference(2) +
  " meters of fence for your dog.");
```

This example shows how to annotate functions and variables.

How it works...

Variables—either standalone or as arguments to a function—are decorated using a colon and then the type. For example, the first function, `greeter`, takes a single argument, person, which must be a string. The second function, `circumference`, takes a radius, which must be a number, and declares a single variable in its scope, `pi`, which must be a number and has the value `3.141592654`.

You declare functions in the normal way as in JavaScript, and then add the type annotation after the function name, again using a colon and the type. So, `greeter` returns a string, and `circumference` returns a number.

There's more...

TypeScript defines the following fundamental type decorators, which map to their underlying JavaScript types:

- `array`: This is a composite type. For example, you can write a list of strings as follows:

  ```
  var list:string[] = [ "one", "two", "three"];
  ```

- `boolean`: This type decorator can contain the values `true` and `false`.

- `number`: This type decorator is like JavaScript itself, can be any floating-point number.

- `string`: This type decorator is a character string.

- `enum`: An enumeration, written with the `enum` keyword, like this:

  ```
  enumColor { Red = 1, Green, Blue };
  var c : Color = Color.Blue;
  ```

- `any`: This type indicates that the variable may be of any type.

- `void`: This type indicates that the value has no type. You'll use `void` to indicate a function that returns nothing.

See also

For a list of the TypeScript types, see the TypeScript handbook at `http://www.typescriptlang.org/Handbook`.

How to declare interfaces using TypeScript

An *interface* defines how something behaves, without defining the implementation. In TypeScript, an interface names a complex type by describing the fields it has. This is known as structural subtyping.

How to do it...

Declaring an interface is a little like declaring a structure or class; you define the fields in the interface, each with its own type, like this:

```
interface Record {
  call: string;
  lat: number;
  lng: number;
}
```

```
Function printLocation(r: Record) {
  console.log(r.call + ': ' + r.lat + ', ' + r.lng);
}

var myObj = {call: 'kf6gpe-7', lat: 21.9749, lng: 159.3686};

printLocation(myObj);
```

How it works...

The `interface` keyword in TypeScript defines an interface; as I already noted, an interface consists of the fields it declares with their types. In this listing, I defined a plain JavaScript object, `myObj` and then called the function `printLocation`, that I previously defined, which takes a `Record`. When calling `printLocation` with `myObj`, the TypeScript compiler checks the fields and types each field and only permits a call to `printLocation` if the object matches the interface.

There's more...

Beware! TypeScript can only provide compile-type checking. What do you think the following code does?

```
interface Record {
  call: string;
  lat: number;
  lng: number;
}

Function printLocation(r: Record) {
  console.log(r.call + ': ' + r.lat + ', ' + r.lng);
}

var myObj = {call: 'kf6gpe-7', lat: 21.9749, lng: 159.3686};
printLocation(myObj);

var json = '{"call":"kf6gpe-7","lat":21.9749}';
var myOtherObj = JSON.parse(json);
printLocation(myOtherObj);
```

First, this compiles with `tsc` just fine. When you run it with node, you'll see the following:

```
kf6gpe-7: 21.9749, 159.3686
kf6gpe-7: 21.9749, undefined
```

What happened? The TypeScript compiler does not add run-time type checking to your code, so you can't impose an interface on a run-time created object that's not a literal. In this example, because the lng field is missing from the JSON, the function can't print it, and prints the value undefined instead.

This doesn't mean that you shouldn't use TypeScript with JSON, however. Type annotations serve a purpose for all readers of the code, be they compilers or people. You can use type annotations to indicate your intent as a developer, and readers of the code can better understand the design and limitation of the code you write.

See also

For more information about interfaces, see the TypeScript documentation at http://www.typescriptlang.org/Handbook#interfaces.

How to declare classes with interfaces using TypeScript

Interfaces let you specify behavior without specifying implementation; classes let you encapsulate implementation details behind an interface. TypeScript classes can encapsulate fields or methods, just as classes in other languages.

How to do it...

Here's an example of our Record structure, this time as a class with an interface:

```
class RecordInterface {
  call: string;
  lat: number;
  lng: number;

  constructor(c: string, la: number, lo: number) {}
  printLocation() {}

}

class Record implements RecordInterface {
  call: string;
  lat: number;
  lng: number;

  constructor(c: string, la: number, lo: number) {
    this.call = c;
```

```
      this.lat = la;
      this.lng = lo;
    }

    printLocation() {
      console.log(this.call + ': ' + this.lat + ', ' + this.lng);
    }
  }

  var myObj : Record = new Record('kf6gpe-7', 21.9749, 159.3686);

  myObj.printLocation();
```

How it works...

The `interface` keyword, again, defines an interface just as the previous section shows. The `class` keyword, which you haven't seen before, implements a class; the optional `implements` keyword indicates that this class implements the interface `RecordInterface`.

Note that the class implementing the interface must have all of the same fields and methods that the interface prescribes; otherwise, it doesn't meet the requirements of the interface. As a result, our `Record` class includes fields for `call`, `lat`, and `lng`, with the same types as in the interface, as well as the methods constructor and `printLocation`.

The constructor method is a special method called when you create a new instance of the class using `new`. Note that with classes, unlike regular objects, the correct way to create them is by using a constructor, rather than just building them up as a collection of fields and values. We do that on the second to the last line of the listing, passing the constructor arguments as function arguments to the class constructor.

See also

There's a lot more you can do with classes, including defining inheritance and creating public and private fields and methods. For more information about classes in TypeScript, see the documentation at `http://www.typescriptlang.org/Handbook#classes`.

Using json2ts to generate TypeScript interfaces from your JSON

This last recipe is more of a tip than a recipe; if you've got some JSON you developed using another programming language or by hand, you can easily create a TypeScript interface for objects to contain the JSON by using Timmy Kokke's json2ts website.

How to do it...

Simply go to `http://json2ts.com` and paste your JSON in the box that appears, and click on the generate TypeScript button. You'll be rewarded with a second text-box that appears and shows you the definition of the TypeScript interface, which you can save as its own file and include in your TypeScript applications.

How it works...

The following figure shows a simple example:

You can save this typescript as its own file, a `definition` file, with the suffix `.d.ts`, and then include the module with your TypeScript using the `import` keyword, like this:

```
import module = require('module');
```

8
Using JSON for Binary Data Transfer

In this chapter, we will discuss the intersection between JSON and binary data. Here, you'll find the following recipes:

- ▶ Encoding binary data as a base64 string using Node.js
- ▶ Decoding binary data from a base64 string using Node.js
- ▶ Encoding and decoding binary data as a base64 string using JavaScript in the browser
- ▶ Encoding data as BSON using Json.NET
- ▶ Decoding data from BSON using Json.NET
- ▶ Using `DataView` to access `ArrayBuffer`
- ▶ Encoding and decoding base64 using an `ArrayBuffer`
- ▶ Compressing object-body content from a Node.js server built using the express module

Introduction

There are typically two reasons why you might want to think about binary representation when using JSON: either because you need to carry binary data between one part of your application to another or because you're worried about the size of the JSON you're transporting.

In the first case, you're actually a little stuck, as the existing JSON specification doesn't provide a container format for binary data because JSON is a text-based representation of data at its heart. You can choose to encode binary data in another format, such as base64, which renders binary data as a printable character string, or you can use an extension of JSON, such as Binary JSON (BSON), that supports Binary data.

BSON uses the semantics of JSON but represents the data in a binary form. Thus, the same basic structure is available: a (possibly nested) map of key-value pairs, where values can be other key-value pairs, arrays, strings, or even binary data. However, instead of using plaintext encoding, the format is binary, which yields a smaller data size and support for binary objects natively (you can learn more about BSON at `http://bsonspec.org/`). The down side to BSON is that it's not natively supported in JavaScript, and being a binary format, isn't amenable to easy inspection. To whet your appetite, I will discuss how to use BSON with the popular Json.NET library in this chapter.

A second approach is to take any binary data and encode it in a format that makes it compatible with text. Base64 is one such encoding mechanism that's been used for a variety of purposes over the years on the Internet, and there's support for it in both modern browsers and Node.js. In this chapter, I show recipes to interconvert with base64 using both the modern browser interfaces and Node.js. Be aware, though, that this means data bloat, because representing binary information as text increases the size of the data being transported.

A common concern people express as they consider JSON for their application is the size of the JSON package in comparison to binary formats such as BSON, protocol buffers, or a hand-tuned binary representation. While JSON can be larger than a binary representation, you gain human readability (especially helpful for debugging), clear semantics, and a large assortment of libraries with working implementations from which to draw. Minimizing whitespace and using short key names can help reduce the size of JSON, as can compression—in a recent project I was working on, my testing showed that compressing the JSON using standard HTTP compression yielded more memory savings than an all-binary representation would have, and was of course easier to implement on both server and clients as well.

Remember that going to binary for the sake of memory—either BSON, compression, or a custom format—negates one of JSON's most useful attributes, which is its property of self-documentation.

Encoding binary data as a base64 string using Node.js

If you have binary data that you need to encode to pass to the client as JSON, you can convert it to base64, a common means on the Internet to represent eight-bit values in solely printable characters. Node.js provides the `Buffer` object and a `base64` encoder and decoder for this task.

How to do it...

First, you'll allocate a buffer, and then you'll convert it to a string, indicating that the string you want should be base64-encoded, like this:

```
var buffer = newBuffer('Hello world');
var string = buffer.toString('base64');
```

How it works...

The Node.js `Buffer` class wraps a collection of octets outside the Node.js V8 runtime heap. It's used in Node.js anytime you need to work with purely binary data. The first line of our example makes a buffer, populating it with the string `Hello world`.

The `Buffer` class includes the `toString` method, which takes a single argument, the means to encode the buffer. Here, we're passing `base64`, indicating that we want `s` to contain the `base64` representation of `b`, but we could just as easily pass one of the following values:

- `ascii`: This value indicates that the high bit should be stripped and the remaining seven bits of each octet converted to their ASCII equivalent.
- `utf8`: This value indicates that it should be encoded as multi-byte Unicode.
- `utf16le`: These are 2 or 4-byte little-endian Unicode characters.
- `hex`: This value is for encoding each octet as two characters, the value in `hex` of the octet.

See also

For documentation on the `Buffer` class of Node.js, see `https://nodejs.org/api/buffer.html`.

Decoding binary data from a base64 string using Node.js

In Node.js, there's no inverse of `Buffer.toString`; instead, you pass the base64 data directly to the buffer constructor, along with a flag indicating that the data is base64 encoded.

Getting ready

If you want to run the example as it appears here, you'll need the `buffertools` module installed, in order to get the `Buffer.compare` method. To get that, run `npm` on a command prompt:

npm install buffertools

If all you're going to do is use the `Buffer` constructor of Node.js to decode `base64` data, you don't need to do this.

How to do it...

Here, we'll take our original buffer and compare it to another one initialized with the original base64 for the first message:

```
require('buffertools').extend();

var buffer = new Buffer('Hello world');
var string = buffer.toString('base64');
console.log(string);

var another = new Buffer('SGVsbG8gd29ybGQ=', 'base64');
console.log(b.compare(another) == 0);
```

How it works...

The first line of the code includes the `buffertools` module, which extends the `Buffer` interface. This is only necessary because I want to use buffer tools's `Buffer.compare` method in the last line; it's not necessary for `base64` to decode itself.

The next two lines create a `Buffer` object and obtain its `base64` representation, which the following line logs to the console.

Finally, I create a second `Buffer` object, initializing it with some base64 data, passing base64 to indicate that the initialization data should be decoded into the buffer. I compare these two buffers on the last line. Note that the buffer tool's `compare` method is an ordinal compare, meaning that it returns 0 if both buffers contain the same data, -1 if the first contains an ordinal sort less than the data, and 1 if the first contains data that would be ordinally sorted as greater.

See also

For information about the `buffertools` module and its implementation, see https://github.com/bnoordhuis/node-buffertools#.

Encoding and decoding binary data as a base64 string using JavaScript in the browser

The base implementation of JavaScript does not include base64 encoding or decoding. However, all modern browsers include the `atob` and `btoa` methods to decode and encode base64 data respectively. These are methods of the window object, defined by the JavaScript runtime.

How to do it...

It's as easy as a method call:

```
var encodedData = window.btoa("Hello world");
var decodedData = window.atob(encodedData);
```

How it works...

The `btoa` function takes a string and returns the base64 encoding of that string. It's a method of the window object and calls to native browser code. The `atob` function does the reverse, taking a string containing base64 and returning a string with the binary data.

See also

For a summary of `btoa` and `atob`, see the Mozilla developer website at `https://developer.mozilla.org/en-US/docs/Web/API/WindowBase64/Base64_encoding_and_decoding` (note that while the documentation is from Mozilla, these methods of `window` are defined by most modern browsers).

Encoding data as BSON using Json.NET

BSON encoding is a reasonable alternative to JSON if you have an implementation of an encoder and decoder on each side of the connection. Unfortunately, there's no good encoder and decoder available yet for JavaScript, but there are implementations for a number of other platforms, including .NET and C++. Let's look at how to encode a class using BSON with Json.NET in C#.

Getting ready

First, you'll need to have the Json.NET assembly available to your application. As you saw in the last chapter, in the recipe *How to deserialize an object using Json.NET*, the easiest way to do this is with NuGet. If you haven't already, add the Json.NET assembly to your solution using the steps in that recipe.

How to do it...

Using Json.NET to encode BSON is fairly simple, once you have a class you want to encode:

```
public class Record {
    public string Callsign { get; set; }
    public double Lat { get; set; }
    public double Lng { get; set; }
```

```
  }
  ...
  var r = new Record {
    Callsign = "kf6gpe-7",
    Lat = 37.047,
    Lng = 122.0325
  };

  var stream = new MemoryStream();
  using (var writer = new Newtonsoft.Json.Bson.BsonWriter(ms))
  {
    var serializer = new Newonsoft.Json.JsonSerializer();
    serializer.Serialize(writer, r);
  }
```

How it works...

It's easiest to start with a class that has the fields that you want to convert, defined, as you'd do for other type-safe conversions from JSON. Here, we define a simple Record class for this purpose and then create a record to encode.

Next, we create MemoryStream to contain the encoded data, and a BsonWriter object to do the writing to the memory stream. Of course, anything that implements the .NET streaming interface will work with the BsonWriter instance; you could write to a file instead if you preferred. After that, we create an actual serializer to do the work, an instance of JsonSerializer, and use it to serialize the record we created using the writer itself. We wrap the actual serialization in a using block, so that at the end of the operation, the resources used by the writer (but not the stream) are immediately cleaned up by the .NET runtime.

See also

Documentation for the BsonWriter class is available from NewtonSoft at http://www.newtonsoft.com/json/help/html/T_Newtonsoft_Json_Bson_BsonWriter.htm.

Decoding data from BSON using Json.NET

Using Json.NET, decoding BSON is the opposite of encoding; given a class that describes the data to decode and a blob of binary data, invoke a reader to read the data.

Getting ready

Of course, you need a reference to the Json.NET assembly in your project in order to do this. See recipe *How to Deserialize an object using Json.NET* in *Chapter 7, Using JSON in a Type-safe Manner*, to learn how to add a reference to Json.NET in your application using NuGet.

How to do it...

Starting with a stream, you'll use a `BsonReader` with a `JsonSerializer` to deserialize the BSON. Assuming data is `byte[]` of BSON data:

```
MemoryStream ms = new MemoryStream(data);
using (var reader = new Newtonsoft.Json.Bson.BsonReader(ms))
{
  var serializer = new Newtonsoft.Json.JsonSerializer();
  var r = serializer.Deserialize<Record>(reader);

  // use r
}
```

How it works...

We create `MemoryStream` from the incoming data, which we use with `BsonReader` to actually read the data from the stream. The reading is done by the `JsonSerializer`, which deserializes using the reader into a new instance of the `Record` class.

There's more...

You may not have a class that represents the data you deserialize in your application; that's often the case early in development, when you're still defining the semantics of your data transfer. You can use the `Deserialize` method to deserialize a `JsonObject` instance, and then use the JsonObject's interface to obtain individual field values. For information about `JsonObject`, see the Json.NET documentation at `http://www.newtonsoft.com/json/help/html/T_Newtonsoft_Json_JsonObjectAttribute.htm`.

See also

The documentation for `BsonReader` from NewtonSoft is at `http://www.newtonsoft.com/json/help/html/T_Newtonsoft_Json_Bson_BsonReader.htm`.

Using a DataView to access an ArrayBuffer

Sometimes, you don't want to work with JSON at all, but instead with pure binary data. JavaScript provides the `DataView` abstraction, which lets you perform typed accesses on an array buffer of memory, such as one obtained from an `XMLHttpRequest` object.

Getting ready

To begin, you need your data in an `ArrayBuffer`, such as the one returned by the `XMLHttpRequest` object. With this, you can create a `DataView`, and then using that `DataArray`, create a typed array over the data view to extract just the bytes that you're interested in. Let's see an example.

How to do it...

Here's a simple example:

```
var req = new XMLHttpRequest();
req.open("GET", url, true);
req.responseType = "arraybuffer";
req.onreadystatechange = function () {
  if (req.readyState == req.DONE) {
    var arrayResponse = req.response;
    var dataView = new DataView(arrayResponse);
    var ints = new Uint32Array(dataView.byteLength / 4);

    // process each int in ints here.

  }
}
req.send();
```

How it works...

The first thing to notice is `responseType` of the `XMLHttpRequest` object. In this example, we're setting it to `arraybuffer`, indicating that we want a raw buffer of bytes back represented as an instance of the `ArrayBuffer` class. We make the request, and on the done handler, create `DataView` of the response.

The `DataView` is an abstraction object from which we can create different views to read and write the binary data to and from the `ArrayBuffer` object.

`DataView` supports viewing `ArrayBuffer` objects as any of the following:

- `Int8Array`: This is an 8-bit two's complement signed integer array

- `Uint8Array`: This is an 8-bit unsigned integer array

- `Int16Array`: This is a 16-bit two's complement signed integer array

- `Uint16Array`: This is a 16-bit unsigned integer array

- `Int32Array`: This is a 32-bit two's complement signed integer array

- `Uint32Array`: This is a 32-bit unsigned integer array

- `Float32Array`: This is a 32-bit floating point number array

- `Float64Array`: This is a 64-bit floating point number array

In addition to constructing one of these arrays from a `DataView`, you can also access individual 8-bit, 16-bit, 32-bit integers, or 32-bit or 64-bit floats from a `DataView`, using a corresponding getter function, passing the offset to the number you want to get. For example, `getInt8` returns `Int8` at the location you specify, while `getFloat64` gets the corresponding 64-bit floating point number at the offset you specify.

See also

Although `ArrayBuffer` and `DataView` aren't specific to Microsoft Internet Explorer, the documentation at Microsoft's MSDN site is very clear. See `https://msdn.microsoft.com/en-us/library/br212463(v=vs.94).aspx` for information about the `DataView` methods, or see `https://msdn.microsoft.com/library/br212485(v=vs.94).aspx` for an overview of typed arrays in general.

Encoding and decoding base64 using an ArrayBuffer

If you're going to use `ArrayBuffer` and `DataView` for your binary data and carry binary data as base64 strings, you can use the Mozilla-written functions at `https://developer.mozilla.org/en-US/docs/Web/API/WindowBase64/Base64_encoding_and_decoding#Solution_.232_.E2.80.93_rewriting_atob%28%29_and_btoa%28%29_using_TypedArrays_and_UTF-8` to do so. They provide the functions `strToUTF8Arr` and `UTF8ArrToStr` to perform UTF-8 encoding and decoding, as well as `base64EncArr` and `base64DecToArr` to convert between base64 strings and array buffers.

How to do it...

Here's an interconversion example that encodes a text string as UTF-8, then converts the text into base64, then shows the base64 results, and finally converts the base64 to `ArrayBuffer` of UTF-8 data before converting the UTF-8 back to a regular character string:

```
var input = "Base 64 example";

var inputAsUTF8 = strToUTF8Arr(input);

var base64 = base64EncArr(inputAsUTF8);

alert(base64);

var outputAsUTF8 = base64DecToArr(base64);

var output = UTF8ArrToStr(outputAsUTF8);

alert(output);
```

How it works...

Mozilla defines four functions in the file on their website:

- ▸ The `base64EncArr` function encodes `ArrayBuffer` of bytes as a base64 string
- ▸ The `base64DecToArr` function decodes a base64 string to `ArrayBuffer` of bytes
- ▸ The `strToUTF8Arr` function encodes a string as an array of UTF-8 encoded characters in `ArrayBuffer`
- ▸ The `UTF8ArrToStr` function takes `ArrayBuffer` of UTF-8 encoded characters and returns the string it encodes

Compressing object-body content from a Node.js server built using the express module

If space is your primary concern when using JSON that has you considering a binary representation, you should seriously consider using compression instead. Compression can yield similar savings to a binary representation, it is implemented with `gzip` in most servers and HTTP clients, and can be added as a transparent layer after you've finished debugging your application. Here, we discuss adding object-body compression for JSON and other objects sent by the popular express server built on top of Node.js with the express module.

Getting ready

First, you need to make sure you've installed the express and compress modules:

npm install express

npm install compression

You could also `npm install -g` it, if you want it to be available to all Node.js applications in your workspace.

How to do it...

When initializing your `express` module in your server's entry point, require compression, and tell `express` to use it:

```
var express = require('express')
var compression = require('compression')
var app = express()
app.use(compression())

// further express setup goes here.
```

For more information on using `express` module to set up a server, see the recipe "Installing the express module for Node.js" in *Chapter 5, Using JSON with MongoDB*.

How it works...

HTTP headers support the client indicating whether or not it can decompress object bodies sent over HTTP, and modern browsers all accept `gzipped` object bodies. By including compress in your server built on express, you make it possible for clients to request compressed JSON as part of their web API requests, and receive compressed JSON in response. No change is necessary in most cases for most clients, although if you're writing a native client with your own HTTP implementation, you may need to check the documentation to determine how to enable `gzip` decompression over HTTP.

The code begins by requiring the express module and compression module, and then configures the express module to optionally use compression if it's requested by the client when sending responses.

9
Querying JSON with JSONPath and LINQ

Sometimes, all you may want to do is extract a field or two from some JSON-formatted data, rather than parse a JSON blob into a class and work with all of its fields. With JSONPath or LINQ (using Json.NET), you can do just that. Here, you'll find the following recipes:

- ▸ Using the JSONPath dot-notation to query JSON documents
- ▸ Using JSONPath bracket-notation to query JSON documents
- ▸ Using JSONPath scripting to construct more complicated queries
- ▸ Using JSONPath in your web application
- ▸ Using JSONPath in your Node.js application
- ▸ Using JSONPath in your PHP application
- ▸ Using JSONPath in your Python application
- ▸ Using JSONPath in your Java application
- ▸ Using JSONPath with SelectToken to query for JSONPath expressions in your C# application
- ▸ Using LINQ with Json.NET to query JSON in your C# application

Introduction

One of the biggest strengths of XML is XPath, the query-oriented language to query subsections of an XML document. Stefan Goessner proposed the JSONPath query language, a language with features similar to XPath that lets you extract just the bits of a JSON document your application needs.

Note that something's still doing the parsing: you don't get something for nothing, and JSONPath implementations require JSON parsing with at least similar memory and runtime characteristics. However, if there's a JSONPath library for the platform you're developing, JSONPath can lead to more readable code, as you don't need to mock entire classes only to extract a field or two or summarize a field across a collection of JSON values.

If you're used to developing for Microsoft platforms, you're certainly aware of Microsoft's **Language Independent Query** (**LINQ**) language that lets you use write declarative queries on enumerable data structures. While the .NET implementations of JSON parsing provide only rudimentary LINQ support, the indomitable Json.NET library's implementation supports LINQ as well as JSONPath, letting you make declarative queries of JSON documents using either fluent or statement syntax.

To use either JSONPath or LINQ, you'll need a library that supports it. As I write this, there are libraries that support JSONPath for JavaScript, the flavour of JavaScript of Node.js, PHP, C#, Python, and Java. Of course, if you want to use LINQ, you'll need to be running your application on the .NET platform using a language such as C#, F#, or Visual Basic. Consequently, most of the recipes that follow have two steps: what to do to download a library that supports JSONPath and then the actual steps to call the JSONPath code in your application.

Most JSONPath examples use Goessner's example document, consisting of records from a hypothetical bookstore, and in this chapter, we'll stick with that example as well. Our JSON document looks like this:

```
{ "store": {
    "book": [
        { "category": "reference",
        "author": "Nigel Rees",
        "title": "Sayings of the Century",
        "price": 8.95
      },
        { "category": "fiction",
        "author": "Evelyn Waugh",
        "title": "Sword of Honour",
        "price": 12.99
      },
        { "category": "fiction",
        "author": "Herman Melville",
        "title": "Moby Dick",
        "isbn": "0-553-21311-3",
        "price": 8.99
      },
        { "category": "fiction",
        "author": "J. R. R. Tolkien",
        "title": "The Lord of the Rings",
        "isbn": "0-395-19395-8",
```

```
        "price": 22.99
      }
    ],
    "bicycle": {
      "color": "red",
      "price": 19.95
    }
  }
}
```

As you can see, we have a store object, which has a collection of books and a single bicycle. Each book has a category, an author, a title, and a price. Representing a JSON document like this as a class would be difficult because of the very different structures of the book records as opposed to the bicycle record; you could use the type-unsafe query methods that we discussed in *Chapter 1, Reading and Writing JSON on the Client*, and *Chapter 2, Reading and Writing JSON on the Server*, to parse a document like this and traverse its document, although a better choice for most applications is JSONPath, as you'll soon see. Let's begin with how to query the document for individual fields.

Using the JSONPath dot-notation to query JSON documents

JSONPath uses *expressions* written in either the dot-notation or bracket-notation to denote a traversal of fields in the JSON document. Dots separate field names, as if they were object attributes.

How to do it...

Here are a few examples of dot-notation:

```
$.store.book[0].title
$.store.book[*].title
$.store..price
$..book[3]
```

How it works...

In the first line, we reference the first (counting from zero) book in the store, returning the title field. The second line is similar, except that it returns a collection of all titles of all the books. The third example returns a collection of all price fields in all records in the store collection. The fourth example finds the fourth book item in the store.

The notation is fairly intuitive, except for the use of .. and *. These are examples of some of the special characters used by JSONPath to denote slices across the document.

There's more...

JSONPath defines the following special characters you can use when writing queries:

▶ The $ symbol refers to the root object or element.

▶ The @ symbol refers to the current object or element.

▶ The . operator is the dot-child operator, which you use to denote a child element of the current element.

▶ The [] operator is the subscript operator, which you use to denote a child element of the current element (by name or index).

▶ The * operator is a wildcard, returning all objects or elements regardless of their names.

▶ The , operator is the union operator, which returns the union of the children or indexes indicated.

▶ The : operator is the array slice operator, so you can slice collections using the syntax [start:end:step] to return a subcollection of a collection.

▶ The () operator lets you pass a script expression in the underlying implementation's script language. It's not supported by every implementation of JSONPath, however.

See also

The definitive JSONPath documentation is available at Goessner's website at http://goessner.net/articles/JsonPath/. Of course, you should check the documentation for the implementation of JSONPath that you choose for specific implementation details.

One handy thing on the Web is a JSONPath expression tester; http://jsonpath. curiousconcept.com/ is one such site. By pasting JSON and a JSONPath expression in the tester, you can evaluate the JSONPath and see what the result is. This is a very easy way to dynamically debug your JSONPath expressions as you first start. Here's an example:

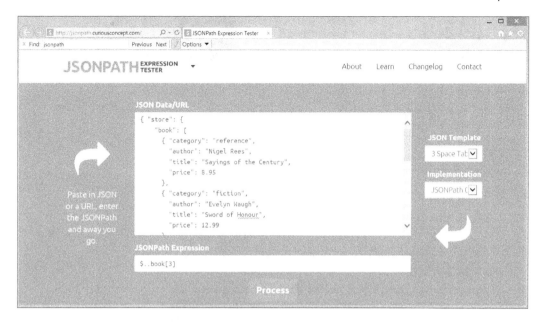

Using JSONPath bracket-notation to query JSON documents

JSONPath provides an alternate notation, bracket-notation, which works just like dot-notation to query fields. The syntax is reminiscent of how you access fields in associative arrays, where you pass the field name as the selector to `operator[]` to obtain the value in the named field.

How to do it...

In bracket notation, we will write the previous recipe's example as follows:

```
$['store']['book'][0].['title']
$['store']['book'][*].['title']
$['store']..['price']
$..['book'][3]
```

How it works...

As seen earlier, the first example extracts the title of the first book in the object in the field named store. The second example extracts all titles of all books in the store. The third example returns a collection of all price fields for every item in the store, and the fourth example returns the fourth book in the store.

Using JSONPath scripting to construct more complicated queries

Sometimes, what you really want to do is query all items that meet a certain criteria, such as those exceed a particular threshold. JSONPath provides the `?()` predicate, which lets you execute simple comparison scripts of individual fields in your JSONPath.

How to do it...

Here's an example that queries all books costing less than `10` currency units:

```
$.store.book[?(@.price < 10)].title
```

How it works...

The query begins by specifying all book items in the store; the `?()` predicate then selects each item in that category using the `@` selector to obtain the value of the current item, and then selects prices less than `10`. The resulting items have their title field extracted. This query yields the following results:

```
[
    "Sayings of the Century",
    "Moby Dick"
]
```

Queries like this don't work with all implementations of JSONPath. Checking the JSONPath Expression tester at `http://jsonpath.curiousconcept.com/`, I found that it worked using the flow communications JSONPath 0.1.1 but not Goessner's implementation of JSONPath in version 0.8.3.

Any expression that returns a Boolean can be used in the `?()` predicate. Here's another example that queries all books in the fiction category in our collection:

```
$.store.book[?(@.category == "fiction")].title
```

The beginning is the same, that is, selecting for all books; instead of filtering by price and returning books costing less than `10`, this returns all items in the collection where a specific item in the book collection has a category field equal to fiction.

Using JSONPath in your web application

Using JSONPathwith JavaScript in your web application is easy. You only need to include the `jsonpath.js` implementation in your application, and then use its `jsonPath` function.

Getting ready

Before you begin, you need to download the JavaScript `jsonpath` library from `https://code.google.com/p/jsonpath/` and include it in the scripts your HTML page uses with a script tag, like this:

```
<html>
<head>
<title>…</title>
<script type="text/javascript" src="jsonpath.js"></script>
</head>
```

The `jsonPath` function takes a JSON object (not as a string, but as a JavaScript object) and applies the path operation to the contents, returning either the matched values or a normalized path. Let's see an example.

How to do it...

Here's an example that returns a list of titles from the JSON object I showed in the introduction:

```
var o = { /* object from the introduction */ };
var result = jsonPath(o, "$..title");
```

Note that if you have the object as a string, you'll have to parse it first using `JSON.parse`:

```
var json = "…";
var o = JSON.parse(json);
var result = jsonPath(o, "$..title");
```

How it works...

The preceding code uses the `jsonPath` function to extract all titles from the currently passed object. The `jsonPath` function takes a JavaScript object, path, and an optional result type that indicates whether the return value should be the value or the path to the value. The incoming object can either be a structured object or an array, of course.

See also

Goessner's original documentation for the original implementation of JSONPath is at `http://goessner.net/articles/JsonPath/`.

Using JSONPath in your Node.js application

There's an npm package available that contains an implementation of the JavaScript JSONPath implementation, so if you want to use JSONPath from Node.js, you only need to install the JSONPath module and call it directly.

Getting ready

To install the JSONPath module, run the following command to include the module in your current application:

```
npm install JSONPath
```

Alternatively, you can run the following command to include it for all projects on your system:

```
npm install -g JSONPath
```

Next, you'll have to require the module in your source code, like this:

```
var jsonPath = require('JSONPath');
```

This loads the JSONPath module into your environment, storing a reference in the jsonPath variable.

How to do it...

The JSONPath module for Node.js defines a single method, eval, which takes a JavaScript object and a path to evaluate. For example, to obtain a list of the titles in our example document, we would need to execute the following code:

```
var jsonPath = require('JSONPath');

var o = { /* object from the introduction */ };
var result = jsonPath.eval(o, "$..title");
```

If you're going to be applying a path to JSON in string form, be sure to parse it first:

```
var jsonPath = require('JSONPath');

var json = "…";
var o = JSON.parse(json);
var result = jsonPath.eval(o, "$..title");
```

How it works...

The `eval` method of the `JSONPath` module takes a JavaScript object (not a string containing JSON) and applies the path you pass to return the corresponding values from the object.

See also

For documentation about the JSONPath module for Node.js, see `https://www.npmjs.com/package/JSONPath`.

Using JSONPath in your PHP application

Using JSONPath in your PHP application requires you to include the JSONPath PHP implementation available at `https://code.google.com/p/jsonpath/`, and parsing the JSON string to a PHP mixed object before applying the JSONPath path you want to extract data from with the `jsonPath` function.

Getting ready

You'll need to download `jsonpath.php` from `code.google.com` at `https://code.google.com/p/jsonpath/` and include it in your application with the `require_once` instruction. You'll also need to ensure that your PHP implementation includes `json_decode`.

How to do it...

Here's a simple example:

```
<html>
<body>
<pre>
<?php
  require_once('jsonpath.php');
  $json = '…'; // from the introduction to this chapter
  $object = json_decode($json);
  $titles = jsonPath($object, "$..title");
  print($titles);
?>
</pre>
</body>
</html>
```

How it works...

The preceding code begins by requiring the PHP JSONPath implementation, which defines the `jsonPath` function. It then decodes the JSON string using `json_decode`, before extracting the titles in the mixed PHP object that `json_decode` returns.

Like the JavaScript version of `jsonPath`, the PHP version takes three arguments: the object from which to perform the extraction, the path to extract, and an optional third argument that specifies whether to return the data or return the path to the data in the structure.

See also

For more information about the PHP implementation of JSONPath, see Stefan Goessner's web site at `http://goessner.net/articles/JsonPath/`.

Using JSONPath in your Python application

There are several implementations of JSONPath for Python, too. The best is `jsonpath-rw` library, which provides language extensions so that paths are first-class language objects.

Getting ready

You'll need to install the `jsonpath-rw` library using pip:

```
pip install jsonpath-rw
```

Also, of course, you will need to include the necessary bits of the library when using them:

```
fromjsonpath_rw import jsonpath, parse
```

How to do it...

Here's a simple example using our store contents in the introduction stored in the variable `object`:

```
>>> object = { … }

>>>path = parse('$..title')

>>> [match.value for match in path.find(object)]
['Sayings of the Century','Sword of Honour', 'Moby Dick',
  'The Lord of the Rings']
```

How it works...

Processing a path expression using this library is a little like matching a regular expression; you parse out the JSONPath expression and then apply it to the Python object you want to slice using path's `find` method. This code defines the object and then creates a path expression storing it in path, parsing the JSONPath that fetches all titles. Finally, creates an array of values found by the path in the object you pass to the path.

See also

The documentation for the Python JSONPath library is at `https://pypi.python.org/pypi/jsonpath-rw`.

Using JSONPath in your Java application

There's an implementation of JSONPath for Java, too, written by **Jayway**. It's available from GitHub, or you can obtain it through the **Central Maven Repository** if your project uses the Maven build system. It matches the original JSONPath API, returning Java objects and collections for fields in JSON objects.

Getting ready

You'll need to either download the code from GitHub at `https://github.com/jayway/JsonPath`, or, if you're using Maven as your build system, include the following dependency:

```
<dependency>
<groupId>com.jayway.jsonpath</groupId>
<artifactId>json-path</artifactId>
<version>2.0.0</version>
</dependency>
```

How to do it...

The Java implementation parses your JSON and exports a `JsonPath` class with a method read that reads JSON, parses it, and then extracts the contents at the path you pass:

```
String json = "...";

List<String>titles = JsonPath.read(json,
"$.store.book[*].title");
```

How it works...

The read method parses the JSON you pass, and then applies the path you pass to extract the values from the JSON. If you have to extract more than one path from the same document, it's best to parse the document only once, and then call read on the parsed document, like this:

```
String json = "...";

Object document =
Configuration.defaultCConfiguration().jsonProvider().parse(json));

List<String>titles = JsonPath.read(document,
  "$.store.book[*].title");
List<String>authors = JsonPath.read(document,
  "$.store.book[*].author");
```

There's more...

The Java JSONPath library also provides a fluent syntax, where the implementation of read and other methods returns a context on which you can continue to invoke other JSONPath library methods. For example, to obtain a list of books with a price more than 10, I can also execute the following code:

```
List<Map<String, Object>>expensiveBooks = JsonPath
                        .using(configuration)
                        .parse(json)
                        .read("$.store.book[?(@.price > 10)]",
                          List.class);
```

This configures JsonPath using the configuration, parses the JSON you pass, and then invokes read with a path selector that selects all book objects with a price greater than the value 10.

The JsonPath library in Java attempts to cast its result objects to the primitive classes you expect: lists, strings, and so forth. Some path operations—.., ?(), and [number:number:number]—always return a list, even if the resulting value is a single object.

See also

For the documentation on the Java JSONPath implementation,
see https://github.com/jayway/JsonPath.

Using JSONPath with SelectToken to query for JSONPath expressions in your C# application

If you use Newonsoft's Json.NET for the .NET environment, you can use its `SelectToken` implementation to make JSONPath queries of JSON documents. First, you'll parse the JSON into `JObject` and then make a query.

Getting ready

You'll need to include the Json.NET assembly in your application. To do this, follow the steps in *Chapter 7, Using JSON in a Type-safe Manner*, in the *Getting ready* section of the *How to Deserialize an object with Json.NET* recipe.

How to do it...

Here's how to extract all titles of all books from the example in the introduction and get the first result:

```csharp
using System;
using System.Collections.Generic;
using System.Linq;
    using Newtonsoft.Json.Linq;

// …

static void Main(string[] args)
{
  var obj = JObject.Parse(json);

  var titles = obj.SelectTokens("$.store.book[*].title");

  Console.WriteLine(titles.First());
}
```

How it works...

The `SelectTokens` method of `JObject` takes a JSONPath expression and applies it to the object. Here, we extract a list of `JObject` instances, one for each item matching the top-level `$.store.book` path, and then invoke the `Values` method to obtain coerced string values for each of the title fields in each of the returned `JObject` instances. Of course, the original JSON needs to be parsed, which we do with `JObject.parse`.

Note that `SelectTokens` returns an enumerable collection, which you can further process using LINQ expressions, as we do here by invoking `First`. Strictly speaking, `SelectTokens` returns `IEnumberable<JToken>`, where each `JToken` is a single JSON collection. JObject also provides the `SelectToken` method, which returns a single instance.

Be careful not to confuse `SelectToken` and `SelectTokens`, however. The former can *only* return a single `JToken`, while the latter is required anytime you want to return a collection of items in your JSONPath query.

Filtering is supported, too. For example, to obtain `JObject` containing the data about the book *Moby Dick*, I might write:

```
var book = obj.SelectToken(
"$.store.book[?(@.title == 'Moby Dick')]");
```

This selects the document with `title` matching `"Moby Dick"` from the `book` collection in the `store` field.

See also

See the documentation and more examples for `SelectToken` and `SelectTokens` at Jason Newton-King's website at `http://james.newtonking.com/archive/2014/02/01/json-net-6-0-release-1-%E2%80%93-jsonpath-and-f-support`, or the Json.NET documentation at `http://www.newtonsoft.com/json/help/html/QueryJsonSelectToken.htm`.

Using LINQ with Json.NET to query JSON in your C# application

If you're developing for .NET, you might just want to skip JSONPath entirely and use Json.NET's support to subscribe based on field name and support for LINQ. Json.NET supports LINQ out of the box, letting you craft any query you want against your JSON in either fluent or statement syntax.

Getting ready

As with the previous recipe, your .NET project needs to use Json.NET. To include Json.NET in your project, follow the steps I show you in *Chapter 7, Using JSON in a Type-safe Manner*, in the *Getting Started* section of the *How to Deserialize an Object with Json.NET* recipe.

How to do it...

You'll parse the JSON to `JObject`, and then you can just evaluate LINQ expressions against the resulting `JObject`, like this:

```
using System;
using System.Collections.Generic;
using System.Linq;
using Newtonsoft.Json.Linq;

static void Main(string[] args)
{
  var obj = JObject.Parse(json);
  var titles = from book in obj["store"]["book"]
      select (string)book["title"];

  Console.WriteLine(titles.First());
}
```

Of course, because it's LINQ, fluent syntax is supported, too:

```
using System;
using System.Collections.Generic;
using System.Linq;
using Newtonsoft.Json.Linq;


static void Main(string[] args)
{
  var sum = obj["store"]["book"]
              .Select(x => x["price"])
              .Values<double>().Sum();

  Console.WriteLine(sum);
}
```

How it works...

The first example selects all `title` objects, one from each `book` field, casting each to a string before returning the result. The second example performs a selection on all `price` fields of `book`, casting the resulting value to a double and invoking `Sum` method on the list to obtain the total price of all of the books.

Something to look out for is that the usual return type of a sub-field in a Json.NET LINQ query is `JObject`, so you have to use the `Value` and `Values` methods of the `JObject` template to obtain the values of those objects when you're writing an expression in fluent syntax. Your first attempt at calculating the sum might have read something like the following:

```
var s = obj["store"]["book"].
   Select(x =>x["price"]).Sum();
```

However, this won't work because the return value of the selection is a list of `JObjects`, which can't be summed directly.

 When writing LINQ expressions, LINQPad (`http://www.linqpad.net`) is especially helpful. If you're doing a lot of LINQ and JSON, investing in the Developer or Premium versions may be wise, as these versions support integration with NuGet that let you include Json.NET right in your test queries.

See also

For more information about LINQ and Json.NET, see the Json.NET documentation at `http://www.newtonsoft.com/json/help/html/LINQtoJSON.htm`.

10
JSON on Mobile Platforms

Mobile applications today are all the rage—devices like tablets and smart phones are outselling PCs in many parts of the world. Powered by platforms such as iOS and Android, these devices include APIs for creating and parsing JSON as part of the platform, making your life as an application developer a little easier. In this chapter are recipes for:

- ▶ Parsing JSON on Android
- ▶ Generating JSON on Android
- ▶ Parsing JSON on iOS in Objective-C
- ▶ Generating JSON on iOS in Objective-C
- ▶ Parsing JSON on iOS using Swift
- ▶ Generating JSON on iOS using Swift
- ▶ Parsing JSON using Qt
- ▶ Generating JSON using Qt

Introduction

As we discussed in previous chapters, JSON is an excellent medium to communicate with web services and clients, whether the clients are web applications or traditional applications. This is especially true for mobile applications, many of which run over lower-bandwidth wide area networks, where JSON's brevity in comparison with XML makes overall data payloads smaller, and thereby ensuring faster response time for remote queries.

Today's leading mobile platforms are Android and iOS. Android, running a variant of Linux, supports software development in Java and includes a JSON processor in the `org.json` namespace. iOS, loosely derived from Mach and BSD, supports software development using Objective-C, Swift, C, and C++, although for most application development, you use Objective-C or Swift, each of which contains a binding to the `NSJSONSerialization` class, which implements JSON parsing and JSON serialization.

An additional option for mobile developers is to use a cross-platform toolkit, such as Qt, for application development. Qt runs on a variety of platforms, including Android, iOS, and BlackBerry. Qt defines the `QJsonDocument` and `QJsonObject` classes, which you can use to interconvert between maps and JSON. Qt is an open source framework that's been around for many years, and runs not just on mobile platforms, but on Mac OS X, Windows, and Linux, as well as many other platforms.

The JSON we'll discuss in the following sections is similar to what we've been using in the past chapters and is a document that looks like this:

```
{
  'call': 'kf6gpe-7',
  'lat': 37.40150,
  'lng': -122.03683
  'result': 'ok'
}
```

In the discussions that follow, I assume that you've correctly set up the software development environment for the platform you're targeting. Describing the process of setting up software environments for Android, iOS, and Qt would take more space than this book allows. If you're interested in developing software for a specific mobile platform, you may want to consult the developer resources for Android or iOS:

▸ You can find Apple's developer site for iOS developers at `https://developer.apple.com`.

▸ You can find Google's developer site for Android developers at `http://developer.android.com/index.html`.

▸ You can find information about Qt at `http://www.qt.io`.

Parsing JSON on Android

Android provides the `JSONObject` class, which lets you represent the name-value pairs of JSON documents through an interface that's conceptually similar to a map, and includes serialization and deserialization through getter and setter methods that access the named fields of a JSON object.

How to do it...

You begin by initializing `JSONObject` with the JSON that you want to parse and then use its various `get` methods to obtain the values of the JSON fields:

```
Import org.json.JSONObject;

String json = "…";
JSONObject data = new JSONObject(data);

String call = data.getString("call");
double lat = data.getDouble("lat");
double lng = data.getDouble("lng");
```

How it works...

The `JSONObject` constructor takes the JSON to parse and provides accessor methods to access the fields of the JSON. Here, we use the `getString` and `getDouble` accessors to access the `call`, `lat`, and `lng` fields of the JSON respectively.

The `JSONObject` class defines the following accessors:

▸ The `get` method, which returns a subclass of `java.lang.Object` containing the value in the named slot.

▸ The `getBoolean` method, which returns a `Boolean` if the slot contains a `Boolean`.

▸ The `getDouble` method, which returns a `double` if the slot contains a `double`.

▸ The `getInt` method, which returns an `int` if the slot contains an `int`.

▸ The `getJSONArray` method, which returns an instance of `JSONArray`, the JSON parsing class that handles arrays, if the slot contains an array.

▸ The `getJSONObject` method, which returns an instance of `JSONObject` if the slot contains another map.

▸ The `getLong` method, which returns a `long` if the slot contains a `long`.

▸ The `getString` method, which returns a `String` if the slot contains a `String`.

The class also defines `has` and `isNull`. These take the name of a slot and return `true` if there's a value in the field name, or if there's no field named or the value is `null` respectively.

`JSONArray` is similar to `JSONObject`, except that it works with arrays and not maps. It has the same getter methods, which take integer indices in the collection, returning objects, Booleans, strings, numbers, and so forth.

There's more...

The `JSONObject` class also defines the `keys` method, which returns `Iterator<String>` of the keys in the JSON. You can also obtain `JSONArray` of the names in the JSON by invoking `names` or the number of key-value pairs in the JSON by invoking `length`.

See also

For more information about `JSONObject`, see the Android documentation at `http://developer.android.com/reference/org/json/JSONObject.html`. For more information about `JSONArray`, see `http://developer.android.com/reference/org/json/JSONArray.html`.

Generating JSON on Android

`JSONObject` also supports setter methods to initialize data in a JSON map. With these methods, you can assign data to a JSON object and then get the JSON representation by invoking its `toString` method.

How to do it...

Here's a simple example:

```
import org.JSON.JSONObject;

JSONObject data = new JSONObject();
data.put("call", "kf6gpe-7");
data.put("lat", 37.40150);
data.put("lng", -122.03683);
String json = data.toString();
```

How it works...

The polymorphic put method can take an integer, long integer, object, Boolean, or double, assigning the slot you name the value you specify.

The `JSONObject` class defines the `toString` method, which takes an optional number of spaces to indent nested structures for pretty-printed JSON. If you don't pass this indent, or pass 0, the implementation encodes the JSON in as compact a manner as possible.

There's more...

There's also the putOpt method, which takes any subclass of Object, and puts the value to the name if both the name and value are non-null.

You can assign a slot an array of values by passing JSONArray or nest maps by passing another JSONObject as the value to be set. JSONArray defines a similar put method, which takes as a first argument the integer index into the array, rather than a slot name. For example, with the data object from the previous example, I could add an array of measured voltages at a station (maybe from the radio's battery) with the following code:

```
import org.JSON.JSONObject;

JSONArray voltages = new JSONArray();
voltages.put(3.1);
voltages.put(3.2);
voltages.put(2.8);
voltages.put(2.6);
data.put("voltages", voltages);
```

You can also put java.util.Collection and java.util.Map instances directly, instead of passing JSONArray or JSONObject instances. The previous code might also be written as:

```
import org.JSON.JSONObject;
import org.JSON.JSONArray;
import java.util.Collection;

Collection<double> voltages = new Collection<double>();
voltages.put(3.1);
voltages.put(3.2);
voltages.put(2.8);
voltages.put(2.6);
data.put("voltages", voltages);
```

This makes life a little easier when constructing more complex JSON objects because you needn't wrap every Java collection or map in a corresponding JSON object.

See also

For more information about JSONObject, see the Android documentation at http://developer.android.com/reference/org/json/JSONObject.html. For more information about JSONArray, see http://developer.android.com/reference/org/json/JSONArray.html.

Parsing JSON on iOS in Objective-C

Objective-C's class libraries define the `NSJSONSerialization` class, which can serialize to and from JSON. It converts JSON to `NSDictionary` objects of values, with the keys, the names of the slots in the JSON, and the values of their JSON. It's available in iOS 5.0 and later.

How to do it...

Here's a simple example:

```
NSError* error;
NSDictionary* data = [ NSJSONSerialization
  JSONObjectWithData: json
  options: kNilOptions
  error: &error ];

NSString* call = [ data ObjectForKey: @"call" ];
```

How it works...

The `NSJSONSerialization` class has a method, `JSONObjectWithData:options:error`, that takes an `NSString`, parsing options, and a place to record errors, and performs JSON parsing. It can accept JSON whose top level is an array or dictionary, returning an `NSArray` or `NSDictionary` result respectively. All values must be instances of `NSString`, `NSNumber`, `NSArray`, `NSDictionary`, or `NSNull` respectively. If the top-level object is an array, the method returns `NSArray`; otherwise, it returns `NSDictionary`.

There's more...

By default, the data that this method returns is non-mutable. If you want mutable data structures, instead, you can pass the option `NSJSONReadingMutableContainers`. To parse top-level fields that are not arrays or dictionaries, pass the option `NSJSONReadingAllowFragments`.

See also

Apple's documentation for the class is at `https://developer.apple.com/library/ ios/documentation/Foundation/Reference/NSJSONSerialization_Class/ index.html`.

Generating JSON on iOS in Objective-C

You can also use the `NSJSONSerializer` class to serialize `NSDictionary` or `NSArray`; simply use the `dataWithJSONObject` method.

How to do it...

Here's a simple example assuming that data is `NSDictionary` you want to convert to JSON:

```
NSError *error;
NSData* jsonData = [NSJSONSerialization
dataWithJSONObject: data
options: NSJSONWritingPrettyPrinted
error: &error];
```

How it works...

The `dataWithJSONObject:options:error` method can take `NSArray` or `NSDictionary` and returns an `NSData` blob with the encoded JSON of the collection you passed. If you pass `kNilOptions`, the JSON will be encoded in a compact manner; for pretty-printed JSON, pass the option `NSJSONWritingPrettyPrinted` instead.

See also

Apple's documentation for the `NSJSONSerialization` class is at `https://developer.apple.com/library/ios/documentation/Foundation/Reference/NSJSONSerialization_Class/index.html`.

Parsing JSON on iOS using Swift

The same `NSJSONSerialization` class is available in Swift, Apple's new language for iOS development.

How to do it...

Here's an example of how to invoke the `JSONObjectWithData` method of `NSJSONSerialization` in Swift:

```
import Foundation
var error: NSError?
Let json: NSData = /* the JSON to parse */
let data = NSJSONSerialization.JSONObjectWithData(json,
  options: nil,
  error: &error);
```

How it works...

Method invocations in Swift look like function invocations, with the arguments passed as (optionally named) comma-delimited arguments, similar to how they're invoked in C++ or Java. The arguments to `JSONObjectWithData` are identical to the method arguments in the Objective-C version.

Generating JSON on iOS using Swift

Of course, you can invoke the `NSJSONSerialization.dataWithJSONObject` method from Swift, too, which returns an `NSData` object that you can then convert to a string.

How to do it...

Here's a simple example:

```
var error: NSError?
var data: NSJSONSerialization.dataWithJSONObject(
   dictionary,
   options: NSJSONWritingOptions(0),
   error: &error);
var json: NSString(data: data, encoding: NSUTF8StringEncoding);
```

How it works...

The method `dataWithJSONObject` operates just as its Objective-C counterpart does. Once we receive `NSData` containing the JSON-encoded version of the dictionary, we convert it to `NSString` using the `NSString` constructor.

Parsing JSON using Qt

The Qt implementation of JSON parsing is actually quite similar in its interface to the Android version. Qt defines the `QJsonObject` and `QJsonArray` classes, which can contain JSON maps and JSON arrays respectively. The parsing itself is done by the `QJsonDocument` class, which has a static `fromJson` method that accepts JSON and performs the necessary parsing.

How to do it...

Here's a simple example:

```
QString json = "{ 'call': 'kf6gpe-7', 'lat': 37.40150, 'lng':
-122.03683, 'result': 'ok'}";
QJsonDocument document = QJsonDocument.fromJson(json);
QJsonObject data = document.object;
QString call = data["call"].toString();
```

How it works...

The parsing is two-step: first, the code parses the JSON using `QJsonDocument` and then uses the resulting `QJsonObject` to access the data.

The `QJsonObject` class works as a map of `QJsonValue` objects, each of which can be converted to their fundamental types using one of the following methods:

- ▸ `toArray`: This method converts to `QJsonArray`
- ▸ `toBool`: This method converts to a Boolean
- ▸ `toDouble`: This method converts to a double
- ▸ `toInt`: This method converts to an integer
- ▸ `toObject`: This method converts to another `QJsonObject`, letting you nest maps of `QJsonObject`
- ▸ `toString`: This method converts to `QString`

There's more...

You can also iterate over the keys in `QJsonObject` using either Qt's `foreach` macro or the `begin`, `constBegin`, and `end` iteration methods. There's also the contain method, which takes a name for a slot and returns true if the map contains the slot you're looking for.

See also

See Qt's documentation on JSON parsing at `http://doc.qt.io/qt-5/json.html`.

Generating JSON using Qt

The `QJsonDocument` class also has the `toJson` method, which converts the object it's referencing to JSON.

How to do it...

Here's an example that converts from JSON and back to JSON, pretty-printing the JSON along the way:

```
QString json = "{ 'call': 'kf6gpe-7', 'lat': 37.40150, 'lng':
   -122.03683, 'result': 'ok'}";
QJsonDocument document = QJsonDocument.fromJson(json);
QJsonObject data = document.object;
QByteArrayprettyPrintedJson =
document.toJson(QJsonDocumented::Indented);
```

How it works...

The QJsonDocument class has a method, toJson, which converts the document or array it's referencing to JSON. You can ask for a pretty-printed version of the JSON by passing QJsonDocument::Indented, or a compact version of the JSON by passing QJsonDcoument::Compact.

See also

For more information on QJsonDocument, see the Qt documentation at http://doc.qt.io/qt-5/qjsondocument.html.

Index

Symbols

$http method
about 65
URL 65

A

accessors, JSONObject class
getBoolean method 157
getDouble method 157
getInt method 157
getJSONArray method 157
getJSONObject method 157
getLong method 157
get method 157
getString method 157
AJAX application
building 32
ajax method
URL 56
Android
JSON, generating on 158, 159
JSON, parsing on 156-158
AngularJS
dependency, adding to web server 62, 63
URL 63
used, for obtaining request progress 67, 68
used, for parsing returned JSON 68, 69
used, for requesting JSON content 64, 65
used, for sending JSON to web server 65, 66
Apache CouchDB wiki
URL 97

Apple's developer site, for iOS developers
URL 156
ArrayBuffer
accessing, DataView used 134
used, for decoding base64 135
used, for encoding base64 135
ArrayBuffer objects, DataView
Float32Array 135
Float64Array 135
Int8Array 135
Int16Array 135
Int32Array 135
Uint8Array 135
Uint16Array 135
Uint32Array 135
asynchronous request
making, for data 36, 37
progress, obtaining of 39-41
atob function
about 131
URL 131
attribute-name-attribute-value property 3
attributes, $http method
data attribute 65
headers attribute 65
method attribute 65
params attribute 65
timeout attribute 65
url attribute 65
Automated Packet Reporting System (APRS)
about 32
URL 32

B

base64
decoding, ArrayBuffer used 135
encoding, ArrayBuffer used 135
binary data
decoding, as base64 string using
JavaScript 130
decoding, from base64 string using
Node.js 129
encoding, as base64 string using
JavaScript 130
encoding, as base64 string using
Node.js 128, 129
BSON
about 128
URL 128
BsonReader documentation
URL 133
BsonWriter class documentation
URL 132
btoa function
about 131
URL 131
Buffer class
ascii 129
hex 129
URL 129
utf8 129
utf16le 129
buffertools module
URL 130

C

C#
about 11
JSON, reading in 11-13
JSON, writing in 11-13
C++
about 7
JSON, reading in 7-10
JSON, writing in 7-10
call field 38
Cascading Style Sheets (CSS) 53
Central Maven Repository 149

class documentation, Apple
URL 160
classes, in TypeScript
URL 125
client page
setting up 33-35
Clojure
about 19
JSON, reading in 19-22
JSON, writing in 19-22
collection 80
Comma Separated Values (CSV) 24
Common Language Runtime (CLR) 19
CouchDB
about 95, 96
installing 96, 97
searching, REST used 107
setting up 96, 97
URL 96
CouchDB records
enumerating, REST used 104-106
CouchDB view API documentation
URL 101
CouchDB wiki
URL 101, 102
Cradle
installing 96, 97
setting up 96, 97
used, for connecting to CouchDB
database 97
used, for creating CouchDB database 98
used, for creating document in CouchDB 99
used, for deleting document in CouchDB 103
used, for searching document in
CouchDB 101, 102
used, for setting up data view in
CouchDB 100, 101
used, for updating document in CouchDB 102

D

data
decoding from BSON, Json.NET
used 132, 133
encoding as BSON, Json.NET used 131, 132

R

readyState field 43
remove method 87
request progress
  obtaining, AngularJS used 67, 68
  obtaining, jQuery used 58, 59
REST
  used, for creating document
      in MongoDB 89-91
  used, for deleting document
      in CouchDB 110, 111
  used, for deleting document
      in MongoDB 92, 93
  used, for enumerating CouchDB
      records 104-106
  used, for searching CouchDB 107
  used, for searching MongoDB 87-89
  used, for updating document
      in MongoDB 91, 92
  used, for upserting document
      in CouchDB 108-110
returned JSON
  parsing 42, 43
  parsing, AngularJS used 68, 69
  parsing, jQuery used 59-61
Ruby
  JSON, reading in 28
  JSON, writing in 28

S

SelectToken documentation
  URL 152
server
  setting up 32, 33
structural subtyping 122
SVN
  URL 14
Swift
  used, for generating JSON on iOS 162
  used, for parsing JSON on iOS 161

T

TypeScript
  used, for annotating simple types 121, 122

  used, for declaring classes
      with interfaces 124, 125
  used, for declaring interfaces 122-124
  using, with Node.js 119, 120
TypeScript interfaces
  generating, json2ts used 125, 126
TypeScript types
  URL 122

U

update method 86

V

variables 121
Visual Studio
  URL 11

W

web API
  URL 2
web application
  JSONPath, using 144, 145
web server
  JSON, sending to 37, 38
web service JSON endpoint
  URL 45
web service request
  issuing, Node.js used 45-47

X

XML
  benefits 139
XMLHttpRequest class
  open method 37
  ready states 43
  send method 37
XMLHttpRequest object
  creating 35, 36
  defining 42

Thank you for buying
JavaScript JSON Cookbook

About Packt Publishing

Packt, pronounced 'packed', published its first book, *Mastering phpMyAdmin for Effective MySQL Management*, in April 2004, and subsequently continued to specialize in publishing highly focused books on specific technologies and solutions.

Our books and publications share the experiences of your fellow IT professionals in adapting and customizing today's systems, applications, and frameworks. Our solution-based books give you the knowledge and power to customize the software and technologies you're using to get the job done. Packt books are more specific and less general than the IT books you have seen in the past. Our unique business model allows us to bring you more focused information, giving you more of what you need to know, and less of what you don't.

Packt is a modern yet unique publishing company that focuses on producing quality, cutting-edge books for communities of developers, administrators, and newbies alike. For more information, please visit our website at www.packtpub.com.

About Packt Open Source

In 2010, Packt launched two new brands, Packt Open Source and Packt Enterprise, in order to continue its focus on specialization. This book is part of the Packt open source brand, home to books published on software built around open source licenses, and offering information to anybody from advanced developers to budding web designers. The Open Source brand also runs Packt's open source Royalty Scheme, by which Packt gives a royalty to each open source project about whose software a book is sold.

Writing for Packt

We welcome all inquiries from people who are interested in authoring. Book proposals should be sent to author@packtpub.com. If your book idea is still at an early stage and you would like to discuss it first before writing a formal book proposal, then please contact us; one of our commissioning editors will get in touch with you.

We're not just looking for published authors; if you have strong technical skills but no writing experience, our experienced editors can help you develop a writing career, or simply get some additional reward for your expertise.

JavaScript and JSON Essentials

ISBN: 978-1-78328-603-4   Paperback: 120 pages

Successfully build advanced JSON-fueled web applications with this practical, hands-on guide

1. Deploy JSON across various domains.

2. Facilitate metadata storage with JSON.

3. Build a practical data-driven web application with JSON.

Swift Essentials

ISBN: 978-17-8439-670-1   Paperback: 228 pages

Get up and running lightning fast with this practical guide to building applications with Swift

1. Rapidly learn how to program Apple's newest programming language, Swift, from the basics through to working applications.

2. Create graphical iOS applications using Xcode and storyboard.

3. Build a network client for GitHub repositories, with full source code on GitHub.

Please check **www.PacktPub.com** for information on our titles

Instant GSON

ISBN: 978-1-78328-203-6 Paperback: 60 pages

Learn to create JSON data from Java objects and implement them in an application with the GSON library

1. Learn something new in an Instant! A short, fast, focused guide delivering immediate results.

2. Convert JAVA Objects to JSON representation and vice versa.

3. Learn about the Field Exclusion strategy.

4. Write your own JSON converter.

Instant jsoup How-to

ISBN: 978-1-78216-799-0 Paperback: 38 pages

Effectively extract and manipulate HTML content with the jsoup library

1. Learn something new in an Instant! A short, fast, focused guide delivering immediate results.

2. Manipulate real-world HTML.

3. Discover all the features supported by the Jsoup library.

4. Learn how to Extract and Validate HTML data.

Please check **www.PacktPub.com** for information on our titles